A2 Sociology
UNIT 6

AQA

Module 6: Crime and Deviance

Tony Lawson

Series Editor: Joan Garrod

Philip Allan Updates, part of the Hodder Education Group, an Hachette Livre UK company, Market Place, Deddington, Oxfordshire OX15 0SE

Orders
Bookpoint Ltd, 130 Milton Park, Abingdon, Oxfordshire, OX14 4SB
tel: 01235 827720
fax: 01235 400454
e-mail: uk.orders@bookpoint.co.uk
Lines are open 9.00 a.m.–5.00 p.m., Monday to Saturday, with a 24-hour message answering service. You can also order through the Philip Allan Updates website: www.philipallan.co.uk

© Philip Allan Updates 2002

ISBN 978-0-86003-733-0

This Guide has been written specifically to support students preparing for the AQA A2 Sociology Unit 6 examination. The content has been neither approved nor endorsed by AQA and remains the sole responsibility of the author.

Typeset by Magnet Harlequin, Oxford
Printed by MPG Books, Bodmin

Philip Allan Updates' policy is to use papers that are natural, renewable and recyclable products and made from wood grown in sustainable forests. The logging and manufacturing processes are expected to conform to the environmental regulations of the country of origin.

Contents

Introduction

■ ■ ■

Content Guidance

■ ■ ■

Questions and Answers

Introduction

About this guide

This unit guide is aimed at students taking the AQA A2 Sociology course. It covers the Module 6 topic **Crime and Deviance**, which is examined within Unit 6 and is one of the two choices for synoptic assessment in the AQA examination. This topic is designed to give you a good understanding of the importance of crime and deviance to individuals and to society as a whole, as well as providing you with opportunities to demonstrate your understanding of the links between crime and deviance, theories, methods and other topics within sociology. There are three sections to this guide:

- **Introduction** — this provides advice on how to use this unit guide, an explanation of the skills required in A2 Sociology and suggestions for effective revision. It concludes with guidance on how to succeed in the unit test.
- **Content Guidance** — this provides you with an overview of what is included in the specification for Crime and Deviance. It is designed to make you aware of what you should know before the unit test.
- **Questions and Answers** — this offers some mock exam questions on crime and deviance for you to try, together with some sample answers at grade-A and grade-C levels. Examiner's comments are included on how marks are awarded.

How to use the guide

To get the best from this guide, you need to use parts of it at different times of the course. From the beginning of your study of crime and deviance, you should refer to the Introduction of the guide and have a look at the Content Guidance section. As you go through the topic, you should refer to the relevant part of the Content Guidance to check on your progress and ensure that you have made the appropriate connections to other parts of the course. To gain full advantage from the Question and Answer section, you should wait until towards the end of your entire A2 course. This is because the questions on crime and deviance are synoptic ones: that is, they are designed to check your understanding of sociology as a whole and not just crime and deviance on its own. You will therefore be required to make connections to sociological theories, to sociological methods and to other substantive topics that you have studied throughout your AS and A2 course. It thus makes sense to attempt the practice questions and to review the answers towards the end of your A2 course. When you are ready to do this, take each of the three parts in one of the questions and, by reading carefully, establish whether the part is aimed at assessing your understanding of the links between crime and deviance and:

- other areas of the specification
- sociological theories
- sociological methods

Then, for each part of the question, identify the specific links that you can make to answer the question set. Having studied the questions carefully, you should attempt to answer each part, without looking first at the example answers given. It is important that you try to do the question without looking at the answers, so that you can use a comparison of your answer and the specimen answers to improve your performance. When you have completed your answer, study the grade-A candidate's answer and identify where you might have made other links. Look carefully at the examiner's comments to see where you might have been able to make other improvements. Do not neglect the importance of the different skills that you have to demonstrate. You should also look at the grade-C answer and, using the examiner's comments as a guide, rewrite the answer so that it would gain an A-grade mark.

These activities are time-consuming and should not be attempted all in one go. Divide up the tasks you have to do into manageable chunks (for example, you might want to analyse the links in questions (a) as a first task, then questions (b) at a later date and so on) and complete the activities over a number of weeks. Keep in mind that, as this will be happening towards the end of the course, you will need to have everything completed in good time for the examination. You will therefore need to know on what date the Unit 6 exam is to be held. You should then be able to fit in these activities with your other revision tasks.

In addition to using the questions to develop your examination skills, you could also use the answers as a source of revision material. Just reading through the grade-A candidate's answers should provide you with useful reminders of important sociological material.

The A2 specification

The aims of the A2 Sociology course are to enable you to:
- acquire knowledge and a critical understanding of contemporary social processes and structures
- appreciate the significance of theoretical and conceptual issues in sociological debate
- understand sociological methodology and a range of research methods
- reflect on your own experience of the social world you live in
- develop skills that enhance your ability to participate more effectively in adult life
- demonstrate a deeper understanding of the connections between the nature of sociological thought, methods of sociological enquiry and substantive sociological topics

This last aim is particularly important for crime and deviance as it expresses the synoptic element of A2, which is central to the examination in the topic of Crime and Deviance.

Examinable skills

A2 Sociology papers are designed to test certain defined skills. These skills are expressed as 'Assessment Objectives' in the specification. You will have already been tested in these Assessment Objectives in your AS Sociology module examinations, but the weighting for each of the two Assessment Objectives (AO1 and AO2) has changed for the A2 Sociology specification. Over the three modules of A2, the proportion of marks given to AO1 (knowledge and understanding) is 40% and for AO2 (identification, analysis, interpretation and evaluation) is 60%. The effect of this is that you have to be able to demonstrate more sophisticated skills of analysis and evaluation at A2 than at AS. You will be required to show a more critical, reflective and evaluative approach to methodological issues, to the nature of sociological enquiry and to sociological debates, based on a broad and diverse range of sources.

In addition, Module 6, of which Crime and Deviance is one of the options, carries slightly more weight (40%) in the A2 part of the examination than Modules 4 (30%) and 5 (30%). This is because Module 6 is assessing the synoptic element of the A-level course. Synoptic assessment is defined as the drawing together of knowledge, understanding and skills learned in different aspects of the course. This means that you will have to make connections to other topics you have studied at both AS and A2, including the core themes (see below). You are also required to link your study of crime and deviance to issues concerning the nature of sociological thought that are identified in AO1 (see below) and to sociological theories.

Assessment Objective 1

AO1 concerns the paired skills of knowledge and understanding. You have to demonstrate clearly to the examiners that you have appropriate, accurate knowledge and a good understanding of the sociological material in the topic you are studying. You will find an account of the basic knowledge in Crime and Deviance in the Content Guidance section. The reason for bringing together knowledge and understanding is that it is not enough to be able to reproduce knowledge learned by rote in the examination. You must also be able to use it in a meaningful way to answer the specific question set. This includes the ability to select the most appropriate information from the range of knowledge that you have. This is particularly important in synoptic assessment, as the whole of the course can be drawn upon to show your command of the connections between the parts of the course. In addition, you have to demonstrate your knowledge and understanding of the core themes of the specification. These are:

- socialisation, culture and identity
- social differentiation, power and stratification

Aspects of these themes are dealt with in various elements of the AS and A2 courses. The themes therefore run through the whole of the course, including the topic of Crime and Deviance. You will see examples of where these are dealt with in both the Content

Guidance and the Question and Answer sections. However, you will also be able to make links to these themes through your consideration of the relationship between crime and deviance and other substantive topics, such as the family or religion.

One of the demands of synoptic assessment is that you make connections between sociological methods and crime and deviance. The specification requires that you have a good knowledge and understanding of a range of sociological methods and sources, and that, in particular, you understand the relationship between theory and methods. This includes the way that sociologists:

- acquire primary and secondary data through observation, asking questions and using documents
- analyse qualitative and quantitative data using appropriate concepts
- design and execute sociological research
- are influenced by ethical considerations

The nature of sociological thought is concerned with both concepts and sociological theories. A requirement of synoptic assessment is that you make the links between these concepts and theories and the substantive area you have chosen to study: in this case, Crime and Deviance. The nature of sociological thought covers:

- social order, social control and social change
- conflict and consensus
- social structure and social action
- macro- and micro- perspectives
- the nature of social facts
- the role of values
- the relationship between sociology and social policy

One of the AO1 skills concerns the quality of written communication and includes the ability to:

- use a style of writing appropriate for transmitting complex information
- use specialist vocabulary such as sociological concepts when appropriate
- use accurate spelling, punctuation and grammar to ensure that the meaning is clear

Assessment Objective 2

Assessment Objective 2 (AO2) covers 'identification, analysis, interpretation and evaluation'. At A2 you will need to be more critical and evaluative than in your AS exams, as more marks are given to AO2 skills than to AO1. You will therefore need to:

- select appropriate pieces of sociological knowledge and arguments, and distinguish between facts and opinion (**identification**)
- break down sociological studies and debates into their component parts — concepts, perspectives, methods, findings, conclusion, strengths and weaknesses (**analysis**)
- examine material such as statistics, tables, graphs and research findings to identify trends and establish their meaning and importance (**interpretation**)

- assess the relevance and importance of sociological studies and debates, conveying their strengths and weaknesses and coming to a conclusion about them (**evaluation**)

Evaluation is a particularly important skill at A2 and you should be constantly asking the questions 'Why should I believe this?', 'What evidence is there for this viewpoint?', 'Are there any counter-arguments?' and 'Who says so?' for every piece of sociological research or approach that you come across. You should therefore try to develop the habit of evaluation as you go through your course. A good way to do this is to establish a minimum of two strengths and two weaknesses for every piece of research or every point of view or sociological perspective that you examine. It is even better if you can come to a conclusion about whether it/they are convincing or not, with your conclusion backed by rational argument and solid sociological research.

The AO2 skills include the ability to:
- organise your arguments coherently
- display an understanding of theoretical debates in sociology
- marshal evidence to support arguments and any conclusions you make

Study skills and revision strategies

Study skills

As you go through your A2 course, you should seek to establish routines of study that will help you specifically with the exciting challenge of sociology. The first set of study skills, however, is basic to all your subjects:
- Develop a consistent way of taking notes, both from your teachers and from your reading. There are various techniques and shorthands you can try, but the important thing is to establish what works best for you and to keep to it consistently.
- Review your notes at regular intervals.
- Produce reduced versions of your notes that will help you to revise later on.
- Practise doing examination questions regularly.
- Do any reading that your teacher asks you to do and try to do some of your own, focusing on what particularly interests you about a topic.
- Keep to the regular homework pattern established by your teachers, handing in work when due.

The second set of study skills pertains to A-level Sociology in a more focused way:
- Try to read a quality newspaper every day or, failing that, at least a quality Sunday newspaper. Newspapers like the *Guardian*, *Independent*, *The Times* or *Observer* are invaluable resources for a whole range of sociological topics. They are also useful for you to practise applying your sociological skills to contemporary news stories and for picking up examples to use in your examination. Use your school or local library as a source of these newspapers.

- Use the internet as often as you can. There are some excellent sites dedicated to A-level Sociology and more general sociological sites that will stretch your sociological imagination.
- Subscribe to *Sociology Review* and access back copies held by your school or college library. It is one of the best sources of contemporary sociological work in the areas you will be examined on.
- Look at television and films that you watch from a sociological point of view and try to apply appropriate concepts to the stories. The least it will do is drive your parents and siblings mad!

The third set of study skills relates to the synoptic element of the examination, and in our case to crime and deviance:

- As you go through your other topics on the course, note in the margins any connections that might be made to the topic of Crime and Deviance. For example, if you are doing the topic of Power and Politics, you might note that crime is an issue of some importance in political debates between the parties.
- As you are doing your Crime and Deviance notes, take care to record where your teacher draws attention to any synoptic links.
- Review your notes and note in the margin where other synoptic links might be. Use different colours for links to other parts of the course, to sociological methods and to sociological theories.

Always carry out the **MOT test** to establish synoptic links at every opportunity. You need to make connections to:

Methods that sociologists use
Other areas of the course
Theories that sociologists employ

Revision strategies

For revision strategies, you should take notice of the following points:

- Before you start your revision, make sure that you are aware of what the awarding body specifies for the examination.
- Organise your revision by establishing a timetable for the 2 months before the examination.
- Be active in your revision strategies. Don't just sit there and read your notes. Try to do exercises and activities that test your AO2 skills.
- Practise 'real' exam questions as often as you can. Look at the answers in this unit guide and use them as exemplars and for improving your own performance.
- Organise your revision so that you are not trying to do it all in the few nights before the exam, and so that you can get a good sleep the night before.
- In the exam, divide your time appropriately for the number of marks and make sure that you attempt all parts of a question asked.

The unit test

Crime and Deviance is a Module 6 topic. This module also contains the topic of Stratification and Differentiation. It is unlikely that you will have covered both topics in your course, but if you have, you must choose only one of the two sections on the examination paper. You have to answer all three parts of the single question in each section. Therefore, having chosen the Crime and Deviance section, you have no choices left — you must answer all parts in that section. This question is worth 20% of the whole A-level qualification and is therefore an important component: 8% of the marks are given to AO1 and 12% to AO2. The question is worth 60 marks in total, with 8 marks given to part (a), 12 marks to part (b) and 40 marks to part (c).

Attached to the question will be a single item of source material. This is designed to help you by providing information on which you may draw to answer the question set. You should always read this material carefully first before attempting to answer the questions. It may provide you with important clues in answering one or more of the parts. When one of the questions refers specifically to the item (e.g. 'With reference to Item A' or 'Using Item A and evidence from any part of the course'), you are *required* to make use of the source material. You should do this as obviously as possible to assist the examiner in identifying where in your answer you have obeyed the instruction. For example, you might write, 'As Item A demonstrates...' or 'The view in Item A suggests that a functionalist approach is most useful...'.

The division of marks between the parts (8, 12 and 40) indicates the time that you should allocate to each element. As you have 1 hour and 30 minutes, you should devote roughly two-thirds of the time — about 60 minutes — to part (c), about 15 minutes to part (b) and about 10 minutes to part (a), leaving 5 minutes for reading through and reviewing at the end. While the balance of AO1 and AO2 marks in part (c) is equal, for parts (a) and (b) AO2 marks are in the majority. For part (a) AO1 is given 3 marks and AO2 5 marks. For part (b) AO1 is given 2 marks and AO2 10 marks. The important thing to remember is that the skills of identification, analysis, interpretation and evaluation are more important in A2 examinations and therefore you must take care to demonstrate them. Pay particular attention to the wording of questions, which provides you with clues as to the particular skills being asked for. Note, however, that you need to provide evidence of knowledge and understanding of material from Crime and Deviance in all parts of the question, so you should not neglect these skills either.

The unique feature of Module 6 is that it assesses your synoptic understanding: that is, your ability to deal with sociology as a whole way of thinking and not just as six separate units of knowledge. Therefore the Crime and Deviance question is about your ability to link issues in Crime and Deviance to:

- **Other areas of the course.** You may be given a free choice as to which other topics you will draw upon because different candidates will have studied different topics. In this case, you should try to use relevant material from as many other topics as you can. However, you may be given specific topics from which to make your links. If this is the case, the topics will all be taken from one other module, so that every candidate will have studied at least one of the topics. You will not then be expected to draw on knowledge from more than one topic.

- **The methodological aspects of studying them.** The focus for your answers here will still be on crime and deviance, but there will be a methodological aspect to be addressed.
- **Theoretical issues.** This will require you to engage with material from crime and deviance, but will ask you to deal with a particular approach or perspective within sociology and the strengths and weaknesses of its approach to the topic. It may also invite you to compare or contrast two different approaches to a specific issue in crime and deviance.

The question on crime and deviance is divided into three parts and each part will focus on one of the three synoptic connections. Each of the three questions will be followed by a sentence that will identify for you the type of linkage (other areas, methods or theory) that should be made in that part of the question. So, the links to the methods aspect, for example, may appear as the 8, 12 or 40-mark question. Over all three parts of the Module 6 question on crime and deviance, the three types of linkage will be addressed.

To see the range of issues that may be examined in this module, we now turn to the Content Guidance section.

Content
Guidance

This section is intended to show you the major issues and themes covered in **Crime and Deviance** and the main links that can be made to other areas of the course, to sociological methods and to sociological theories. You must remember, though, that these are offered as guidance only. The points included are not exhaustive — that is, other perfectly legitimate points may be raised by you. You will find many other concepts and studies that are relevant to your exploration of crime and deviance. The main studies in crime and deviance are well rehearsed in all the major textbooks, so you should have no trouble finding them. Your teacher will also give you other studies during your course. The main magazine for A-level sociologists (*Sociology Review*) has focused repeatedly on the issues of crime and deviance, so back copies, available from your school or college library, will be a useful source of information.

The content of Crime and Deviance falls into five main areas:
- **perspectives on crime and deviance**
- **power, crime and deviance**
- **explanations of the social distribution of crime and deviance**
- **the social construction of crime and deviance**
- **the sociological study of suicide**

The AQA A2 topic of Crime and Deviance is designed to give you a comprehensive understanding of the importance of these areas in contemporary societies.
- You will be expected to be familiar with the major sociological explanations of crime and deviance, which include cultural and subcultural theories, control theories, interactionist approaches, conflict and Marxist approaches, left and right realist explanations, and perhaps even some postmodernism!
- You will also need to be aware of the role and activities of the criminal justice system and its agents in the police and courts, as well as the political and legal dimensions, in relation to crime and deviance.
- The social distribution of crime and deviance is another important area of study and covers distribution according to the social characteristics of age, social class, ethnicity, gender and locality.
- For the social construction of crime, you will need to examine how the official statistics of crime and deviance are collected and reported, as well as specifically considering the role of the mass media in the social reaction to criminal and deviant actions. This last point constitutes an obvious synoptic link, as, if you have studied the Mass Media topic, you will be directly relating the issue of crime and deviance to a topic from AS Module 1.
- The issue of suicide has always been one of immense interest to sociologists, as it seems to be the most individual of acts and you will have to explore the socio-logical aspects of suicide.

When you have covered all these areas, you will have completed the topic (and the course!). During your study of crime and deviance, you will need to identify when the two core themes of Culture, Identity and Socialisation, and Stratification, Power and Differentiation are being addressed, as part of your synoptic understanding.

Perspectives on crime and deviance

Sociocultural tradition (Chicago School, strain and subculture theory)

Key ideas

Chicago School

- Patterns of crime in cities are not random.
- The highest levels of crime are found in areas of highest social disorganisation.
- These would be located in 'zones of transition', where there are high rates of migration and divorce, poor housing and communal facilities, family instability and unemployment.
- Such areas retain high levels of disorder, even though the population may change through internal migration.
- Social control of delinquents is easier where there are dense communal networks, and therefore high levels of 'incivility' (a lack of interest in the locality) are associated with high rates of offending.
- Different levels of favourable and unfavourable attitudes to the law and the police in particular urban areas will lead to differential crime rates.

Strain theory

- In mainstream society, there are agreed goals towards which individuals are taught to strive and legitimate means to achieve them.
- Where there is 'strain' between goals and means, deviant activity emerges.
- Deviant and criminal activity can take several forms depending on the nature of the strain, ranging from retreatism (e.g. dropping out) to innovation (e.g. thieving).
- Strain may be experienced not just in economic life, but in personal life as well, such as the loss of a loved one.

Subculture theory

- Those who are non-achievers in mainstream society develop an alternative subculture based on hedonism and machismo.
- Delinquent subcultures are linked to illegitimate opportunity structures, present in the zone of transition.
- Alternative subcultures exist in the inner city, from the retreatist subculture of the drug-taker to the conflict subculture of the gang.
- The lower class has focal concerns that emphasise masculinity and excitement, which lead members into risk-taking and non-conforming behaviour.
- Socialisation into narrow family and peer networks brings individuals into conflict

with the wider society, but contact with these wider networks, such as school or community, decreases the incidence of delinquent behaviour.

Evaluation

+ The Chicago School established the city, and especially the inner city, as a focal point for research into crime and disorder.
+ The concept of social disorganisation is statistically linked with areas of high official crime rates.
+ Strain theory established a societal context for the study of crime and deviance.
+ Strain theory suggests a variety of responses to situations of frustration, not just criminal activity.
+ Subcultural theory established the importance of group norms and values as generators of pro- and anti-crime attitudes.
+ Subcultural theory offers an account of deviance/crime that is located within the participants' own terms of reference and understanding.
− The Chicago School assumes a degree of homogeneity in inner-city communities that is not always easy to show.
− The Chicago School takes the official statistics of offending as the 'true' picture of crime, when much crime in other areas of the city goes undetected.
− Strain theory assumes that there is a general consensus about legitimate goals in society.
− Strain theory does not spell out why any one individual becomes a retreatist rather than a rebel, for example.
− Subcultural theory focuses exclusively on delinquent boys and ignores phenomena such as female gangs.
− It has been difficult to show empirically the existence of distinctive subcultures within inner-city areas.
− All of these theories tend to assume that most crime is committed by the lower classes and ignore white-collar and other types of crimes of the powerful.

Synoptic links

To other areas of the course

The Chicago School was interested in the 'passing on' of pro- and anti-crime attitudes through socialisation in the family — the 'primary level' of socialisation. Both strain theory and subculture theory focused on the inner-city working-class male as the main perpetrator of crime, which has implications for policing in a class-stratified society.

To methodological issues

The Chicago School established a methodological tradition based on the collection of empirical data, combined with 'appreciative sociology' that allowed those investigated to tell their own stories. This was an early combination of quantitative and qualitative measures.

To theoretical issues

Though a relatively 'old' theory of crime, the Chicago School influence can be seen in the growth of 'environmental criminology', which advocates 'target-hardening' strategies to make it more difficult for crimes to be committed. The followers of the Chicago School, strain theory and subculture theory therefore tended to adopt a positivistic approach to the study of crime and deviance.

Key concepts

Zone of transition, social disorganisation, incivility, differential association, strain, conformity, retreatism, innovation, rebellion, ritualism, status frustration, focal concerns, network analysis.

Key thinkers

Park and Burgess, Shaw and McKay, Sampson and Groves, Sutherland, Merton, Cloward and Ohlin, Miller, Bartol and Bartol.

Control theory

Key ideas

- Basic human nature is selfish, with the result that everyone would commit crime if they could get away with it, in order to satisfy their needs.
- Crime therefore results when the individual lacks self-control or where there are insufficient social controls to ensure conformity from individuals.
- Inner containment to prevent criminal actions includes attachment to family, strong orientation towards legitimate goals and psychological predispositions.
- Outer containment includes attachment to community, strong identity with peers and reinforcement of identity by others.
- The social bonds that an individual has (or does not have) are central in explaining conformity (or criminality).
- As individuals grow older, the social bonds they have intensify (e.g. having a family of their own) and so commitment to criminality weakens.
- Criminals lack self-control in many areas of social life, such as in smoking or drug taking, and their decision to commit a crime results from both poor self-control and the presentation of an opportunity to engage in a crime, with minimal risk.
- Society can reduce criminal activity by making it more difficult for opportunist criminals to target their victims.

Evaluation

+ Control theory looks at the pressures to conform in society and the social control arrangements needed to reduce levels of crime.
+ It insists that individuals are making choices when they commit deviant or criminal acts and are not 'forced' to do them.
+ Target-hardening policies are popular with those who live in areas of high crime.
− Control theory assumes that everybody would commit crime if given the chance to do so without detection, but this cannot be shown to be so.
− It over-emphasises the commitment of individuals to deviant activity, which is, more often than not, a transitory, episodic action.

– It seems to suggest that the middle class have more self-control than the working class.

Synoptic links

To other areas of the course

The focus of self-control is on the family and the socialisation process. Control theorists see the lack of a stable home environment and the absence of a strong moral upbringing as resulting in weak inner containment. Parents who do not establish clear lines of child behaviour are responsible for later delinquency.

To methodological issues

Much control theory relies on self-report studies and there are doubts about the validity of the findings of these. Some of the factors in the concept of inner containment are difficult to operationalise and explore.

To theoretical issues

Control theory is often linked to Durkheimian and functionalist sociology because they share a pessimistic view of human nature, seeing men and women as basically out for their individual selves, and therefore needing some strong social pressures to keep them law abiding.

Key concepts

Techniques of neutralisation, inner containment, outer containment, social bonds, power-control theory, self-control theory, administrative criminology.

Key thinkers

Reckless, Hirschi, Hagan, Gottfredson and Hirschi, Coleman.

Interactionist theories

Key ideas

- The activities of the law and the social control agencies such as the police and the courts are central in shaping the pattern of crime and deviance in society.
- Everyone breaks the law, but only certain individuals and groups are targeted by the police and courts to be labelled as criminal or deviant.
- Society reacts to those so labelled differently from the rest of the population.
- Once labelled, the criminal or deviant begins to act in ways that confirm the label.
- Choices made by the police over where to patrol, whom to stop and search, whom to arrest and whom to move to prosecution are important aspects of the operation of micro-power and shape the pattern of apparent criminal activity that emerges.
- Those labelled criminals are not inevitably cast out from mainstream society — in areas of strong communities, shame can be used to reintegrate the offending individual into society.

- Phenomenologists emphasise the meaning of crime for the individuals who commit crimes, focusing on the sense of excitement that they report while engaging in illegal activity.

Evaluation

+ Interactionist theories focus attention on the role of the agents of social control in the 'production' of deviance.
+ They establish the relative nature of the definition of crime and deviance.
+ They see official statistics as socially constructed.
+ Phenomenological approaches show the importance of not just relying on 'official' accounts of deviant/criminal behaviour.
− Interactionist theories tend to trivialise serious deviant/criminal activity such as murder or rape.
− They minimise the importance of the initial deviant/criminal act.
− Not all labelling is counterproductive — it can act to have an opposite effect.
− They ignore structural and ideological processes that shape the responses of society and the social control agencies to particular activities.

Synoptic links

To other areas of the course

Labelling is an important process in the education system as well, suggesting that those labelled successes or failures tend to conform to their teachers' expectations of attainment, depending upon the label attached.

To methodological issues

Labelling is not easy to investigate empirically, as it is difficult to establish the importance of factors that lead to an individual's self-image. It is also difficult to identify primary deviants because, by definition, those who come to the sociologist's attention as 'criminal' have to be secondary deviants.

Participant observation is the interactionist's preferred method and this has many difficulties, not least of which is whether two observers interpret the same events in different ways.

To theoretical issues

The interactionist approach adopted by labelling theorists leads to a lack of consideration of structural issues that might influence the distribution of deviance. Interactionists would argue against the existence of structures in society, focusing only on the meanings and intentions of individuals themselves. Structuralists argue that this is to neglect some deeper processes at work in society that are important in explaining the existence and distribution of crime/deviance.

Key concepts

Labelling, primary deviance, secondary deviance, self-fulfilling prophecy, master status, ecological bias, reintegrative shaming.

Key thinkers

Becker, Lemert, Sampson, Braithwaite, Katz.

Conflict theories

Key ideas

- The poor commit crimes as part of the struggle to live in an unfair capitalist society that dominates their lives, while the rich commit crimes to further their interests in a capitalist society that demands they acquire as much wealth as possible, under the ethic of individualism.
- Capitalism is crimogenic — the ultimate cause of all the criminal activity in society.
- Capitalism generates a surplus population, who are of no economic use to the system and who turn to crime in response to their situation of being outcasts.
- Left idealists see criminals as the victims of capitalism — forced into activity defined as illegal by those who hold power in society, in order to survive.
- Laws under capitalism are created in favour of the dominant social forces and are administered with a bias against subordinate groups in society.
- Criminal law is the product of an alliance between corporate business and the state.
- All deviance and crime has a political dimension and 'crime waves' are often used as a distracting device to focus the population's attention away from capitalism's economic crises.
- Deviant youth subcultures are a way for working-class youth to 'rebel' against the system through adopting 'styles' disapproved of by mainstream society.

Evaluation

- + Conflict theories highlight the macro-influences on crime and deviance, both ideological and economic.
- + They have a focus on law making as well as law breaking.
- + They examine the way in which the choices of the social control agencies are influenced by dominant ideologies of who constitutes the criminal.
- − They ignore the role of law in protecting all members of society, not just the powerful.
- − Socialist societies also had high levels of crime.
- − Left idealism tends to romanticise the deviant and criminal at the expense of the victim.

Synoptic links

To other areas of the course

The issues of economic power and control are important in a number of other areas, not just crime and deviance. In particular, the way that social class is created and reproduced under capitalism and the subordinate position of the working class are important in understanding the apparent concentration of crime in the lower classes. The unequal distribution of wealth and income are also seen in the Marxist analysis of crime and deviance as significant factors in the generation of material crimes.

To methodological issues

The use of content analysis of both media products and semiotic interpretation of 'styles' by conflict theorists has been an important contribution to understanding the role of the media in promoting images and ideologies associated with deviant and criminal subcultures.

To theoretical issues

The role of crime and deviance in supporting or undermining capitalist societies is an issue much discussed in the Marxist approach to crime. For example, Marxists see homosexuality as stigmatised because it represents a 'threat' to the reproduction of the next generation of workers, needed for the survival of capitalism.

Key concepts

Crimogenic, economic determination, selective law enforcement, resistance through rituals, bricolage.

Key thinkers

Quinney, Chambliss, Taylor, Hall, Centre for Contemporary Cultural Studies.

Left realist theory

Key ideas

- The study of crime must be true to the reality of crime and thus focus on the activities of working-class criminals in relation to their mainly working-class victims.
- The focus of investigation in the sociology of crime must be on four 'players' — the activities of the police, the public, the criminal and the victim.
- Crime is concentrated amongst the lower class because members of this group are more likely to be marginalised from society and subject to relative deprivation.
- Marginalisation and relative deprivation vary over time and so crime rates will also vary.
- As the routines of individuals and groups change, so will their potential exposure to the risk of crime: for example, more women going out to work increases women's chances of being victims.
- Relative deprivation, rather than absolute poverty, is an important motivator towards crime, as people feel resentment at those better off than themselves and do not have the possibilities to move forward.
- Working-class subcultures, especially those that emphasise masculinity and risk taking, are also, in the broadest sense, factors in the motivation to crime.
- These factors do not just lead to economic crime, but to other forms of criminality and deviance, such as drug taking and domestic violence.
- The task of left-inclined sociologists is to offer practical programmes to the victims of crime, mainly in the working class, and in the form of self-help and community-based programmes.

Evaluation

+ Left realism focuses attention on the working-class victims of much working-class criminal activity.
+ It insists that the 'fear of crime' is an important aspect of social living.
+ It re-establishes issues of policing as an important dimension of the sociology of crime and deviance.
+ It offers an economic context for crime.
− It does not explore non-working-class crime in any serious way.
− It assumes that it is easy to identify criminals and non-criminals in working-class communities.
− It tends to dismiss female criminality.
− It is idealistic about working-class communities controlling their own criminal element.

Synoptic links

To other areas of the course

Because of the focus on the economic factors of marginalisation and relative deprivation, links can be made to the topic of Wealth, Poverty and Welfare here.

To methodological issues

Many left realist studies are based on small-scale victim surveys carried out in the inner city.

Some critics argue that, although they listen carefully to the 'voices' of the victims of crime, they overlay these with their own interpretation of what is going on, without reference to the victims' points of view.

To theoretical issues

While the left realists reject the more idealistic views of the left idealists and the more condemnatory views of the New Right, they are still optimistic about the chances of controlling crime, through the political activity of the working class. This can be criticised as a naïve view, which tends to see the working class through rose-tinted glasses.

Key concepts

The square of crime, the fear of crime, routine activities theory, marginalisation, relative deprivation, subcultures of masculinity.

Key thinkers

Young, Matthews, Lea, Cohen and Felson, Currie.

Right realist theory

Key ideas

- There is a consensus in society that people and property should be protected against wrong-doing.

- The state has an obligation to deter criminality and punish offenders.
- Traditional values, such as the belief in a strong nuclear family, help to prevent criminal behaviour.
- Individuals have biological predispositions to risk taking and therefore to criminality.
- Individuals make the choice to commit or not to commit crime, based on their predispositions and a calculation of the rewards and penalties that might arise from committing a crime.
- Those most likely to give in to their biological dispositions to crime are to be found in the underclass, where traditional family forms and therefore socialisation into moral codes are weakest.
- The welfare state has weakened the interest of members of the underclass in legitimate employment, and they have therefore turned to illegal activity as a source of income.
- Crime prevention should focus on the opportunities to commit crime, making the effort to commit crime much harder and the penalties associated with it much stiffer.

Evaluation

+ Right realism accords with 'commonsense' thinking about the leniency of the courts towards criminals.
+ It situates criminal actions within the choices that individuals make to commit or not to commit crime.
+ It is critical of explanations of criminality that 'excuse' criminal behaviour.
+ It offers clear advice on the direction of criminal justice policy.
− It is not always obvious what 'traditional values' are.
− Right realism is a populist rather than a sociological approach.
− It is based on crude biological determinism.
− It ignores socioeconomic influences on crime and deviance.

Synoptic links

To other areas of the course
The focus of the New Right on the family is central to understanding their explanations of crime and deviance. It is a particular form of the family (lone parents) that is seen by the New Right as the defining characteristic of an underclass whose members habitually engage in criminal or deviant behaviour.

To methodological issues
The concepts that the New Right employ in relation to their investigations have often been criticised as vague and difficult to operationalise. For example, the 'approval of peers', used in considerations of macho underclass culture, is hard to explore empirically. Rather, the concepts are attacked as constructs, used to justify a particular ideological position.

To theoretical issues
The ideas of the New Right have provoked much controversy amongst sociologists.

Some see them as a necessary counterbalance to the idealism of conflict theories, while others argue that they represent a political position that uses victims as scapegoats for phenomena of which the theorists morally disapprove.

Key concepts
Re-moralisation, constitutional factors, situational criminology, rational choice theory, underclass, welfare dependency.

Key thinkers
Marsland, Wilson and Herrnstein, Cornish and Clarke, James Q. Wilson, Murray.

Postmodern theory

Key ideas

- The underclass in postmodern societies has been cut off from mainstream society, as unemployment and the decline of the welfare state have reduced their reasons for commitment to society.
- As mainstream society rejects the 'discourse of progress' and leaves the underclass to its own devices, the underclass loses all stake in obeying the law.
- In postmodern societies, the inability of many to satisfy their material needs, in a society dominated by consumerism, leads to an 'intensification of resentment' against those who can.
- Crime for the individual becomes a possibility when they feel themselves to have no ties of obligation to the individuals they are targeting.
- Discourses that deny others their humanity are important in creating a climate in which actions that might harm those individuals are made acceptable.
- Social control in postmodern societies is achieved through seduction (being attracted by the consumerism of postmodernity) or repression (of those who do not share in the consumer society).
- The rise of new technologies has made the surveillance and control of the population easier, as individuals practise a form of self-surveillance.
- Postmodern societies are characterised by the extension of the microtechniques of surveillance into our everyday lives, through the routine activities of bureaucracies such as schools.

Evaluation
+ Postmodern theory focuses attention on informal justice within localities.
+ It emphasises that state power is everywhere all the time for everyone, not just in response to criminal activity by wrong-doers.
+ It sees language/discourse as the main way that societies shape what can and cannot be done.
+ It can explain contemporary developments such as dope testing, consumer tracking and speed cameras.
− Postmodernist developments have not been empirically tested, in the main.

- The relativism of postmodernism undermines notions of 'right' and 'wrong' that traditionally underpin criminology.
- Processes whereby discourses play out in society are not always described, but assumed.
- Self-surveillance has yet to be demonstrated as empirically grounded.

Synoptic links

To other areas of the course

Issues of culture are very important to postmodern sociologists and the notion of 'lifestyles' has been used by them to categorise different segments of the population. This has a bearing on issues of crime and deviance, where the pursuit of a deviant or criminal lifestyle can be seen as a choice made by individuals in particular situations.

To methodological issues

The lack of empirical grounding for much of the work of postmodernism is only partly due to its relatively recent development. The ideas that postmodernists put forward are difficult to put into practice in the real world. So, while they have a resonance with the *Zeitgeist* of the early twenty-first century, the evidence for their importance has yet to be confirmed.

To theoretical issues

The challenge of postmodernism to traditional forms of sociology is one of the main theoretical debates going on in sociology, and crime and deviance forms an important arena for debate. This is because the ideas associated with postmodernism have been explored in this area more than others, as the idea of a disciplinary society is so central to postmodernism's case.

Key concepts

Discourse of progress, intensification of resentment, seduction, repression, surveillance, biopower, disciplinary society.

Key thinkers

Morrison, Denzin, Henry and Milovanovic, Bauman, Foucault.

Power, crime and deviance

Crimes of the powerful

Key ideas

- Crime and deviance are spread fairly evenly throughout the class structure; it is just that lower-class offenders tend to be caught and processed as criminals more than middle-class workers are.

- White-collar crime (committed by middle-class workers) merges into corporate crime.
- Occupational crime is that committed by white-collar workers for personal gain; corporate crime is illegal activity commissioned by individuals for corporate gain.
- White-collar crime causes large financial losses to organisations, but is relatively under-investigated by the social control agencies.
- Much corporate crime is extremely harmful to individuals and communities, and is committed because of pressure on executives to cut costs and therefore corners, in order to maximise profits.
- The boundary between organised crime and respectable large corporations is becoming increasingly blurred.
- Corporate crime is increasingly taking on a global dimension as organisations gain the ability to move large amounts of money, staff and expertise swiftly around the world.
- Governments also commit crimes, and increasingly so, and yet human rights legislation has gained legitimacy in many countries. This contradiction is a feature of globalisation.

Evaluation

+ The idea of crimes of the powerful redresses the balance by drawing attention to criminal activity other than that of the working class.
+ It offers a fuller account of the distribution of criminal activity in society.
+ It promotes the investigation of events that may have powerful negative effects on individuals and communities.
− There is a tendency to exaggerate the extent and the effects of corporate crime.
− It is argued that there are strong social and legal pressures on business executives not to commit crimes.
− Corporate crimes in particular are hard to explore with any degree of direct evidence, due to the secretive nature of most corporations.

Synoptic links

To other areas of the course
The illegal activities of corporate bodies can be linked to the study of work and leisure. Most studies in the sociology of work tend to focus on the routine activities of organisations, and the theorists of corporate crime are suggesting that many executives routinely commit criminal acts in the pursuit of profit.

To methodological issues
There are immense difficulties in penetrating the activities of corporations, even when investigating legal activities. For a consideration of their illegal activities, sociologists have to rely mainly on secondary data, such as media stories and government reports, and for primary data may rely on 'whistle-blowers', who have their own methodological difficulties. Those who report the illegal activities of others may have their own motivations for doing so, other than a desire to see the law upheld. They may be jealous, vengeful, ambitious or driven by ideology, for example.

To theoretical issues

While many of the sociologists investigating white-collar crime are drawn from the functionalist tradition of sociology, those interested in corporate crime are usually associated with conflict and Marxist approaches. There are consequently dangers of bias in these approaches.

Key concepts

White-collar crime, corporate crime, occupational crime, state criminality, amoral calculators.

Key thinkers

Sutherland, Coleman, Buss, Chambliss, Kramer, Pearce and Tombs.

Police, crime and deviance

Key ideas

- The police have enormous power in society, but the norms of policing lead to 'under-enforcement' as officers use their powers of discretion to 'keep the peace' rather than just 'enforce the law'.
- 'Cop culture' shapes the ways in which the police deal with different segments of the public and is sometimes accused of being sexist, racist and homophobic.
- The policing policy adopted (community policing, rapid response, paramilitary policing, zero tolerance) is important in defining who gets targeted and how suspects are treated once apprehended.
- Policing tends to be concentrated on members of the underclass and the places where they live, as cop culture identifies the poor as the most law-breaking section of the community.
- Policing activities are not always cost-effective in the fight against crime, as there is a symbiotic relationship between police and crime.
- A major role of the police continues to be the maintenance of social order rather than just catching criminals.
- The privatisation of security is a feature of postmodern societies, as private firms become involved in activities traditionally carried out by the state.
- Police retain considerable symbolic power in society, often seen as a bulwark against disorder and anarchy.

Evaluation

+ The police retain the affection of the public in the fight against crime.
+ The police do respond to the mood of the public for different forms of policing.
+ The everyday activities of the police are multifaceted and varied.
− Differential policing of communities leads to feelings of oppression amongst the most policed.
− Cop culture discourages the participation of women, ethnic minorities and gays in the policing of society.
− Privatised security firms are not subject to the same controls as are the police.

Synoptic links

To other areas of the course

Being a member of the police force is an occupation like any other, and the notion of an occupational culture, drawn from the sociology of work, is important in explaining how the police go about their work.

To methodological issues

The investigation of the activities of the police is affected by many ethical considerations. While there are many television programmes devoted to fictional and real policing, sociologists find that it is hard to carry out observation of real police activities because of the involvement of the criminal and victim in their interactions.

To theoretical issues

The investigation of policing has been carried out by many different types of sociologist, who have focused on different aspects, depending on their theoretical point of view. So, functionalists are interested in the value consensus of the police as they go about their work, while conflict theorists are more focused on police relationships to subordinate communities.

Key concepts

Cop culture, zero tolerance, community policing, privatisation of policing, police voice.

Key thinkers

Banton, Chambliss, Skogan, Morgan, Reiner, Wilson and Kelling.

Law, crime and deviance

Key ideas

- Law is seen by conflict theorists as a key way in which powerful groups in society seek to maintain their hold over less powerful groups.
- Marxists argue that law is directly a tool of the ruling class, used to criminalise those sections of society that might challenge its control and to legitimate its own actions in the pursuit of profit.
- Law for the functionalists represents the accumulated wisdom of the society, which is passed on from generation to generation.
- Postmodernists argue that the law is always a transient set of rules, which is distributed throughout the whole of social life and not just contained in the legal system.
- The law is only one part of a surveillance society.
- The notion of the law can also act as an ideology, used to justify the actions of governments and their agents in defence of it.
- The New Right sees the law as the central means of controlling the activities of a criminal underclass.

Evaluation

+ Sociologists link the law to other social and economic systems, rather than treating it as a separate entity.
+ The role of the law in maintaining social order and establishing social control is established.
+ Postmodernists show that the law is only one of a large number of ways in which power can be expressed in postmodern societies.
− Marxists offer a 'conspiracy theory' of the law, in indicating that it serves mainly the interests of the ruling class.
− Functionalists assume that the law represents wisdom, rather than being the outcome of struggle between different interests in society.
− The law is not just ideological, but also represents a material practice in society associated with ideas such as justice and fairness.

Synoptic links

To other areas of the course

The law frames much of social life: for example, religions are regulated through the law, which establishes the Church of England as the Church of the British state and sets the limits of acceptable religious practice for all religions and sects, such as through its defence of monogamy.

To methodological issues

The law is represented as an abstract body of knowledge and is therefore largely open to investigation only through secondary materials.

To theoretical issues

The divisions between different perspectives on the role of the law stand as an exemplar of the disputes that characterise sociological approaches. Each sociological perspective has its unique view of the nature and function of the law.

Key concepts

Ideological construction, law-and-order ideology, law as a weapon, justice.

Key thinkers

Turk, Scraton, Cavadino and Dignan, Moore.

The criminal justice system, crime and deviance

Key ideas

- The courts and prison service are responsive to changes in public attitudes towards crime and criminals, but also retain a distinctive view of the nature of justice and punishment.

- The criminal justice system is increasingly influenced by the concept of 'risk' in determining its policies towards convicted criminals.
- Criminal justice agencies in a postmodern society classify populations, rather than individuals, as highly likely to commit crime, as the state seeks to control society in an increasingly fractured and disordered world.
- Marxists see the prison system as a source of cheap labour and as a reserve army, with correspondence between the organisation of factories and the organisation of prisons.
- Foucauldian approaches see new initiatives in punishment policies (towards less imprisonment and more community sentencing) as more subtle ways of establishing control over dissident populations.
- Half-way punishments such as community sentences have the effect of widening the net for those caught up in the criminal justice system, as they constitute a cheaper way of punishing offenders than a prison sentence.
- There is a new punitiveness in public attitudes towards punishment, as a result of media highlighting 'crime waves' and an increased fear of crime.
- Incapacitation theory argues that putting people in prison does not deter, but it prevents them from offending while they are inside and this is sufficient justification for incarceration.

Evaluation

+ The focus on the criminal justice system is relatively new and fills a gap in our understanding of crime and deviance.
+ It encompasses a number of central issues in contemporary society, such as justice and punishment.
+ It is linked to practical ideas for improving the efficiency of the criminal justice system and combating crime.
− It tends to assert the importance of the idea of risk rather than showing it to be important.
− Policies to do with prison that are put forward can have real and detrimental effects without necessarily being shown to reduce crime.
− Issues of cost-effectiveness are often to the forefront of these debates, rather than effectiveness in reducing criminal activity.

Synoptic links

To other areas of the course

The Marxist approach argues for a clear correspondence between factories and prisons, while Foucauldians argue that the routines of the prison are diffusing throughout the rest of society in a seamless web of power.

To methodological issues

Studies of criminal justice tend to rely on secondary sources, such as court reports or media accounts of events, because it is, for example, very difficult to gain first-hand experience of prisons.

To theoretical issues

Debates about these issues often take place at a level of high abstraction and principles, so there is always a danger of subjectivity entering into the debate.

Key concepts

New punitiveness, correspondence, risk society, incarceration, incapacitation theory, actuarial justice.

Key thinkers

Ericson, Melossi and Pavarini, Spierenburg, Cohen, Rusche and Kirchheimer, Moore.

Explanations of the social distribution of crime and deviance

Social class

Key ideas

- The official statistics on crime represent a real concentration of criminal activity in the working class and a relative absence of criminal behaviour amongst the middle and upper classes.
- Explanations for this distribution include:
  - The material and social conditions of the working class, including levels of employment, material deprivation and marginalisation from mainstream society.
  - A focus on the characteristics of the working class themselves, including the norms and values they hold, such as hedonism, a search for excitement and machismo.
  - A subculture of risk taking and positive attitudes towards breaking the law and poor socialisation into moral constraints against law breaking.
  - Weak levels of control, in terms of both individual self-control amongst working-class criminals and social control — the penalties used to punish wrong-doing.
  - The demise of working-class communities with strong communal links that acted to deter potential law-breakers.
  - Capitalism, which generates economic outcasts (often unemployed) who have to turn to crime to survive in a hostile world.
  - The activities of the social control agencies, which stigmatise the working class and produce statistics that bear little relation to the real distribution of crime.

- Increasingly, crime is concentrated in an 'underclass' of the 'undeserving poor', characterised by lone parent families, poor socialisation and the collapse of traditional moral values.
- The levels of violence and other deviant/criminal activity, such as drug taking, are significantly higher amongst the lower classes.

Evaluation

+ Official statistics consistently demonstrate that most crime is carried out by lower-class individuals on other lower-class individuals.
+ The focus on social class allows a concentration of resources on those areas most subject to criminal and deviant activity.
+ A combination of factors could explain this concentration and help develop social policies to deal with the problem.
− The emphasis on the working class allows society to turn a blind eye to criminal activity in other social classes.
− Several of the explanations come close to 'victim blaming' and stigmatising large sections of the working class, when the great majority are law abiding.
− The distribution of deviant activity such as drug taking is ubiquitous, not class concentrated, but the target of policing these issues is on the working class.

Synoptic links

To other areas of the course
There are clear links between stratification theories and the focus of research in crime and deviance on the working class. It is the subordinate position of the working class in both material and ideological terms that partly accounts for the way in which it is targeted by sociologists.

To methodological issues
Studies that rely on official statistics for their examination of the class distribution of crime and deviance have to contend with the fact that they are socially constructed, and also that they consistently show that crime is concentrated in a certain class, both as perpetrators and as victims.

To theoretical issues
Different explanations are drawn from different traditions within sociology, so that interactionists do not see the 'crime and class' problem in the same way that Marxists do. The influence of the domain assumptions of these approaches needs to be explored in looking at crime and deviance.

Key concepts

Culture, subculture, material conditions, marginalisation, control, labelling, policing policies, capitalism as crimogenic.

Key thinkers

Braithwaite, Shaw and McKay, Miller, Wolfgang and Ferracuti, Taylor, Morrison.

Age

Key ideas

- Crime and deviant activities are mainly carried out by the young, especially those between 14 and 24, and the majority of victims are also in the same age bracket.
- The main interest of young people is self-gratification, which can lead to feelings of indifference to others, even those who are the potential victims of their actions.
- Not all young people are deviant or criminal and much depends on the strength of their personal networks, such as family, peers, school and community, which connect them to mainstream society. The stronger the bonds, the less likely that the young will be involved in criminal actions.
- Those who do commit crime or deviant acts employ 'techniques of neutralisation' that allow them to suspend their normal commitment to obeying the law, through 'explaining away' their actions.
- Being involved in criminal or deviant activity requires a calculation by the young that the material gain, or the excitement of feeling in control, outweighs the potential of discovery and capture by the agents of social control.
- While most young criminals 'grow out' of their illegal activities, as they settle down to family responsibilities, they continue to demonstrate a lack of self-control in their lives, through heavy drinking, for example.
- Young 'rebels' against the system form deviant subcultures that express their opposition to mainstream society through particular styles, often designed to shock or express difference.
- The lifestyles of the young are likely to expose them to greater risk of victimisation, or offer greater opportunity for them to engage in deviant or criminal behaviour.

Evaluation

- + The focus on the young reflects the statistical and commonsensical views of where crime and deviance are concentrated.
- + Explanations seek to establish both the opportunities for young people to engage in illegal activity and their motivations to do so, in the context of the social situation they find themselves in.
- + Changes over time are included as theorists seek to explain the transition of the young from being at the margins of society to adopting mainstream lifestyles.
- − The focus on the young leads to a neglect of the criminality of other age groups.
- − Much illegal activity of the young is transitory, opportunistic and mundane.
- − 'Rebellion' is a 'natural' (not a deviant) condition for young people as they seek to establish their own identities.

Synoptic links

To other areas of the course

Young people, in various guises or subcultural styles, often form a folk devil for older people. Their stigmatisation is based on nostalgia for a 'lost world' of order and conformity, which has never actually existed. This yearning for a stable past is reinforced through media representations.

To methodological issues

For sociologists, who tend to be slightly older than the young people they are investigating, gaining entry to the social worlds of the latter can be problematic. Several sociologists have secured membership of young people's gangs, but the validity and reliability of the data they have collected are open to debate.

To theoretical issues

While most perspectives offer different views on the causes and consequences of young people's engagement in criminal activity, they seem at first sight to be united in assuming that there is a concentration of criminality in the young. The importance of this (whether it is transitory or deep-seated, mundane or serious) is what separates these perspectives.

Key concepts

Moral symmetry, network analysis, techniques of neutralisation, deviant subculture, style.

Key thinkers

Hough and Mayhew, Schwendinger and Schwendinger, Bartol and Bartol, Box, Matza, Gottfredson and Hirschi, Centre for Contemporary Cultural Studies.

Locality

Key ideas

- Cities are the main locality for the commissioning of crime, while rural areas remain relatively 'crime-free'.
- Certain areas of cities exhibit social characteristics associated with high levels of crime and deviance, such as high levels of geographical mobility, family instability, unemployment and poor living accommodation.
- In urban areas with existing adult criminal enterprises, young people are more likely to engage in crime themselves. In areas without such illegitimate opportunities, young people drift into gang activity or retreatist subcultures based around drugs.
- Cities generate an underclass who have rejected the discourse of progress and who therefore pose a major threat to social order in the city, either through their criminal activity or by their propensity to engage in social disorder.
- Urban crime increases as globalisation dissolves the city's manufacturing base, which constitutes the basis for community life in inner-city areas.
- Poor urban communities lose the sense of space and identity traditionally associated with the inner city, as warehouses and industrial land are given over to expensive flats and gentrification.

- Deindustrialisation of the city creates a group of long-term isolated males, who turn to burglary and violence to replace the welfare benefits that have been squeezed by successive governments.

Evaluation

- + There are clear correlations between certain urban areas and levels of crime.
- + The focus on locality addresses the concentration of poor conditions in certain areas of cities as a cause of crime.
- + It looks at global developments and their effect on urban localities.
- − It is based on a too rigid dichotomy between urban and rural areas.
- − Not all areas with high levels of social disorganisation exhibit high crime rates.
- − The pattern of crime in urban areas is related as much to the pattern of policing as to a greater propensity to commit crime, i.e. individuals in the inner city are more likely to get caught.

Synoptic links

To other areas of the course

There is an important connection to be made between studies of crime and deviance in urban areas and the study of community values and practices. It is the absence of a sense of community in urban areas that is often seen as one of the causes of criminal activity.

To methodological issues

The relationship of global processes to local developments is one that involves a high level of sociological imagination in making the connections between the two levels, as well as a detailed analysis of developments in the world economy and events in small localities.

To theoretical issues

The increased fracturing of cities has been one of the main interests of postmodern sociologists, who are attracted to the idea of a dissolving, uncertain, diverse environment such as the city as a metaphor for postmodern living.

Key concepts

Social disorganisation, illegitimate opportunity structures, retreatism, globalisation, deindustrialisation.

Key thinkers

Park, Burgess, Shaw and McKay, Cloward and Ohlin, Morrison, Petras and Davenport.

Gender

Key ideas

- The apparently lower incidence of crime amongst women cannot be explained solely in terms of biological differences between men and women.
- Explanations of this phenomenon have included the following:

- Girls are differently socialised from boys to accept a more passive, less risk-taking public persona.
- Women do not have the same freedoms in society as men and therefore have fewer opportunities to commit crime.
- The social penalties for deviant behaviour (such as getting pregnant while young) are much greater for women than for men.
- Women have a greater awareness of the risk of arrest and therefore calculate avoidance strategies.
- Crime amongst women is claimed to be rising for the following reasons:
  - Changes in the social roles of women have led to an 'equality of opportunity' to commit crime.
  - Feminism has transformed the way that women see themselves and their needs, so that they are more inclined to seek gratification of material wants through illegal activity.
  - The marginal position of women in the economic market place makes them more predisposed to economic crimes, particularly ethnic minority women.
- Women are more likely to be the victims of crime than perpetrators and are particularly vulnerable to sexual and domestic violence.
- Women commit different types of crime from men, being more likely to shoplift, for example.
- Some argue that it is not that women are less criminally inclined, but that the way the statistics are compiled, and the way that the police and the courts deal with women offenders, lead to a greater invisibility of female crime.
- A focus on masculinity suggests that images of being male are under pressure as the traditional bread-winning role of the man is reduced, leading to a crisis in masculinity that manifests itself in greater violence.

Evaluation

+ The focus on gender reduces the invisibility of women on the sociological agenda.
+ It recognises the importance of female experiences both as criminals and as victims.
+ It locates explanations in the social and ideological relationships in society.
− Explanations of gender and crime have to be tied in with factors such as social class and ethnicity, if there is going to be a full understanding of the issues.
− Focusing on gender tends to treat the female experience as an undifferentiated whole, rather than seeing different groups of women having different experiences of crime and deviance.
− Work on masculinity is undeveloped.

Synoptic links

To other areas of the course

Clearly, this focus on women, men, crime and deviance has a part to play in looking at gender differences in society, in terms of the theme of stratification and differentiation.

To methodological issues

The idea of the invisibility of women from sociological discourse has been paralleled by female absence from empirical studies. Only relatively recently have feminists begun to define what a feminist methodology would look like and how it would be employed to explore the female experience of crime.

To theoretical issues

Feminism as a perspective is one of the most important approaches to the study of female crime and deviance, and you should be aware of the different strands within it, and how each has approached the issues.

Key concepts

Patriarchy, sex role, public/private spheres, malestream sociology, hegemony, hegemonic masculinities.

Key thinkers

Sutherland, Leonard, Steffensmeier and Allen, Heidensohn, Messerschmidt.

Ethnicity

Key ideas

- The relationship between crime rates and ethnicity is extremely complex, due to complicating factors such as the difficulties of identifying ethnic origin and the cultural and social differences between ethnic groups.
- Ethnic minority males are over-represented in the crime statistics, compared to their proportion in the population, and this has been explained by a number of factors:
  - One view suggests that there is a greater disposition towards crime among ethnic minorities for varied reasons.
  - Others argue that the activities of the police target ethnic minorities more, leading to greater arrest rates amongst these groups.
  - A third view suggests that racist stereotypes in cop culture have the effect of over-representing ethnic minorities in arrest figures.
- Explanations for 'black criminality' include the following:
  - The greater economic deprivation of ethnic communities leads to frustration, greater levels of violence and crime.
  - The social isolation by residential segregation of some ethnic communities from mainstream society leads to the development of a subculture that is more disposed to crime.
  - The lack of community networks leads to unsupervised ethnic youth activity, which can lean towards the deviant and criminal.
- Public, police and judicial bias against ethnic minorities ensures that there are hostile encounters with those ethnic minorities caught in criminal justice

processes, such that outcomes are more likely to result in blacks being labelled as criminals.

- Ethnic minorities comprise a large proportion of the underclass, with a concentration effect, so that the social control of the urban environment where they live is seen as necessary for public order.
- The lack of social capital in the form of strong community links can undermine communal censure of drug taking, with the result that there are high levels of use amongst ethnic minorities.
- Ethnic minorities are also more likely to be the victims of crime disproportionately to their numbers, and this is particularly so for ethnic minority women.

Evaluation

+ The focus on ethnicity allows a consideration of the differential experience of ethnic groups in society.
+ There is recognition that there is a complex relationship between the statistics of 'black crime' and the reality on the streets.
+ It identifies drugs and violence as problems for ethnic communities themselves.
− There is a danger that ethnic minorities may be seen as 'naturally' disposed towards crime.
− Research in this area may reinforce the more negative stereotypes that the ethnic minorities and the police may have of each other.
− It is difficult to isolate the effects of the various factors that interplay in the study of ethnicity and crime and deviance.

Synoptic links

To other areas of the course
Ethnicity, along with class and gender, forms the backbone of the theme of stratification and differentiation, which runs throughout the specification. In addition, the issues of culture and identity (the second theme) are also important in seeking to explain the statistics of crime and deviance.

To methodological issues
The lumping together of very different social groups into a single category ('Black' or 'ethnic minority') results in a distortion of the social reality of the various components. This methodological issue has implications for social policy and the way that ethnic minorities are seen by agents of social control.

To theoretical issues
The study of ethnicity is closely tied in to differing perspectives, ranging from the assimilationist views current in the 1960s, through the multicultural perspectives of the 1970s and the anti-racist views of the 1980s, to ideas about new racism in the 1990s.

Key concepts

Hard policing, racism, cop culture, marginalisation, Other, new racism.

Key thinkers

Taylor, Lea and Young, Gilroy, Wilson, Sampson and Laub, Arrigo.

The social construction of crime and deviance

Definitions of crime and deviance

Key ideas

- The notion of deviance presupposes the existence of a 'normality' that most people would subscribe to, and would recognise as such.
- Crime is sometimes defined as a subset of deviance in that all criminal actions are seen as deviant, but not all deviant acts are illegal. However, even some crimes, such as smuggling a few cigarettes through customs, are largely accepted as not deviant.
- Even what is constituted as crime varies through time and space, with different societies having different notions of criminal actions and each society constantly changing its laws.
- Both crime and deviance are subject to social construction: that is, social processes that affect the inclusion or non-inclusion of actions as either deviant or criminal.
- Categories like deviant are subject to discourses (ways of thinking and speaking about what is possible to do and what is not), such as scientific, moral and legal discourses, which change our conceptions of activities depending on the dominant discourse.
- Definitions of crime have been extended to include the concept of the victim as an important player in the phenomenon of crime.

Evaluation

+ There is a flexible approach to definitions that allows social change to be accounted for.
+ The categories of crime and deviance would be readily recognised by individuals, even if they could not agree on a definition.
+ We need to have definitions of crime in order to explore the causes of it and attempt to offer some solutions.
− It is argued that the category of deviance can have no meaning in a social world suffused with difference.
− The relativism of the category of crime in terms of time and space means that there can be little overall agreement on its causes.
− Some would argue that the above two points render the whole of the sociology of crime and deviance as pointless.

Synoptic links

To other areas of the course
The definitional problems of crime and deviance are echoed in other areas of the course: for example, when looking at the ways in which religion might be defined and

the implications that different definitions have for the questions that sociologists ask about it.

To methodological issues

When asking respondents about their attitudes towards crime and deviance, sociologists tend to assume that they all share a common understanding of what crime and deviance are. However, it is not always the case that there are common definitions amongst respondents, and therefore they may be responding to questions with a different conception in mind.

To theoretical issues

The problem of relativism is a central one in sociological debates. The important aspect is whether the dependency of a concept's definition on a particular time and place makes discussion of the phenomenon pointless or not.

Key concepts

Relativism, consensus, difference, social censure, normality, social construction, scientific discourse.

Key thinkers

Durkheim, Sumner, Sykes, Hagan, Sparks.

Official statistics

Key ideas

- Official statistics on crime are used extensively by sociologists as indicators of the amount and type of crime and the background of offenders, even though the statistics cannot represent the 'real' rate of crime.
- Much crime is invisible because crimes are under-reported for a number of reasons, including the following:
  - Victims sometimes do not know a crime has been committed against them.
  - Victims sometimes decide not to report a crime because of embarrassment or the trivial nature of the crime.
  - The police may decide to deal with a crime unofficially rather than officially.
  - Some crimes, especially financial frauds or deceptions, are difficult to detect.
- Discretionary powers of the police and Crown Prosecution Service mean that many known crimes are not processed through the courts, but remain at the level of cautions or informal actions.
- Official statistics on crime are therefore subject to processes of social construction, in which social control agencies (mainly the police and the courts), victims, perpetrators and the public all have a role.
- Even where the statistics are accepted as robust, there are difficulties in interpreting them reliably.

- As laws change, public opinion about acceptable and unacceptable behaviour varies and there are fluctuations in the statistics that are the product of social forces other than just the rate of crime: for example, changes in policing practices.
- Self-report and victim surveys suggest higher rates of crime than the official statistics, though these are also not without their problems.

Evaluation

+ The official statistics provide a ready-made resource for sociologists interested in crime.
+ They show sufficient regularities and patterns across time to demonstrate something about the extent of reported crime.
+ They are used as guides for the formation of social policy in relation to crime by governments and social control agencies.
− The use of official statistics introduces systematic bias into the study of crime, stigmatising lower-class ethnic males in the inner city and ignoring huge amounts of white-collar crime.
− The social construction of such statistics means that they do not describe the real rate of crime and can lead to a fear of crime that is unrelated to an individual's real risk of becoming a victim.
− Statistical correlations between crime and social factors can lead to simplistic explanations of the causes of crime and inappropriate measures to combat it.

Synoptic links

To other areas of the course

The use of official statistics in many areas of sociology is a matter of controversy. Such statistics as birth and death rates are seen as 'hard' statistics — that is, robust and valid — while those to do with religious attendance are seen as 'soft'. Crime statistics, like the unemployment rate, are somewhere between these two.

To methodological issues

The use of official statistics to measure social phenomena is fraught with difficulty, and yet they are a most useful tool in describing and analysing large-scale trends and phenomena in society.

To theoretical issues

Positivists are most likely to accept that the official statistics of crime represent a real social phenomenon worthy of sociological investigation, while interactionists would be more interested in the processes that lead to the social construction of the statistics and would reject the idea that they represented anything 'real'.

Key concepts

Patterned regularities, bias, social construction, under-reporting, invisibility, selective law enforcement, self-report studies.

Key thinkers

Mirrlees-Black, Box, Morrison, Croall.

Deviancy amplification

Key ideas

- Most people's perceptions of crime are obtained from media reports.
- There is a tendency for the media to sensationalise events and unusual social groups, so that they come to be seen by the public as folk devils: that is, as a phenomenon about which 'something must be done'.
- The reactions of the social control agencies to this moral panic lead to over-policing, with the effect that more criminal activity by the social group is detected.
- Those labelled as folk devils often play up to their image in the media, thus creating a self-fulfilling prophecy of a dangerous deviant group.
- The spiral of events, exaggeration and reaction continues until the media lose interest in the group or the focus shifts to other sensational events.
- The more complex structure of the media (with the growth of the internet etc.) makes the establishment of folk devils more problematic because of the variety of sources of information.
- However, social reality for the majority is shaped by the way that the media mediate information about the wider social world.

Evaluation

- + Deviancy amplification is a useful model for exploring the issues of 'crime waves' and the 'fear of crime'.
- + It establishes the centrality of the media as a source of information and imagery about events and people beyond the individual's immediate experience.
- + It links the forces of social control with both the public and members of the deviant subcultures.
- − Those who seek to influence the course of public debate about a social group or social issue are much more diverse than just the media, though most will engage with the media as they seek to persuade the public of the rightness of their views.
- − Members of deviant subcultures have a more complex relationship with the media, often using them to spread knowledge about their lifestyle choices.
- − Unless there is real concern in the general public about an issue, then scapegoating is difficult to accomplish.

Synoptic links

To other areas of the course

The obvious link in this section is to the mass media, which operates as the main vehicle for deviancy amplification.

To methodological issues

One of the main methodological techniques used by sociologists of deviancy amplification is content analyses of media reports. They chart the rise and portrayal of folk devils in the media, and compare them to the public response to the representations depicted.

To theoretical issues

The notion of deviancy amplification emerges firmly from the interactionist school of sociology and particularly from work on labelling. Realist critics of this approach suggest that it implies that the actions of the folk devils are in some sense harmless or trivial, even when they include violence.

Key concepts

Folk devils, moral panics, stereotyping, stigmatisation, media representation.

Key thinkers

Cohen, McRobbie and Thornton, Taylor.

The sociological study of suicide

The Durkheimian tradition and suicide

Key ideas

- The most individual of all acts, the taking of one's own life, is subject to social influences, which have a real existence beyond the individual.
- Suicide is defined as any action or inaction that directly or indirectly leads to the individual taking his or her own life.
- Durkheim rejected both biological (hereditary) and psychological explanations of the suicide rate.
- Some individuals are more prone to suicidal acts than others, but the force that determines the rate of suicide is social and related to the amount of integration or regulation in society.
- Too much or too little regulation and too much or too little integration lead to different forms of suicide.
- Later Durkheimians relate the suicide rate to the stability of social relationships in society, with lower-status integration leading to higher suicide rates.
- Refinements of Durkheim's theories tend to simplify the fourfold division of suicide because of the difficulty in separating out altruistic, fatalistic, egoistic and anomic acts.

Evaluation

+ Durkheimian theory established a specifically sociological view of the individual.
+ It explains different suicide rates in different countries by reference to their social characteristics.
+ It emphasises the power of social forces in shaping individual lives.
− It denies the importance of individual choice in the act of suicide.

– It does not explain why suicidogenic impulses are translated into suicide in some predisposed individuals and not others.
– Suicide statistics are themselves open to question about their validity.

Synoptic links

To other areas of the course

Durkheim's starting point was the 'problem of order': that is, how do individuals, with all their selfishness, manage to live together in society? This is one of the fundamental questions in any discussion of power and politics.

To methodological issues

The use of official statistics as a basis for explaining the incidence of suicide in different societies has been subject to a great deal of methodological scrutiny, with the conclusion that, while they do seem to show patterned regularities with remarkable consistency, they are subject to social construction processes.

To theoretical issues

Durkheim's insistence on the real existence of social forces has provoked much debate, with interactionists in particular seeing this as a reification of society.

Key concepts

Regulation, integration, suicidogenic impulse, altruism, anomie, fatalism, egoism, reification.

Key thinkers

Durkheim, Gibbs and Martin, Ginsberg.

Ecological approaches

Key ideas

- Developed out of the Chicago School tradition, this argues that there is an 'urban trend' in the suicide rate, with cities showing consistently greater incidence of suicide than rural areas.
- Comparing different areas of the city shows consistently high levels of suicide in localities with the characteristics of social disorganisation.
- Indicators such as high levels of rented accommodation, divorce and pawn shops are related to high levels of suicide.
- Inner-city areas have concentrations of individuals with the highest level of personal disorganisation, who are more likely to seek to take their own lives.
- It is therefore not poverty that, of itself, leads people to commit suicide in these areas, but mobility and the lack of social cohesion and community, which might make those who could withstand disruption within a strong community turn to suicide as a way out.
- Unemployment is a factor because becoming unemployed also means being cut adrift from the work community, and a loss of resources that enable individuals to participate fully in communal life.

Evaluation

+ This approach focuses on the nature of community life as an explanation for differential suicide rates.
+ It recognises the importance of economic factors in explaining high rates of suicide, by including unemployment as a factor.
+ It involves an element of social change in its theory, by insisting upon the rate of growth of cities, rather than just size, as the important dimension.
− There is a danger of an ecological fallacy: that is, the inadmissibility of reading from the general characteristics of a population as a whole (all those in an area) to a constituent group within it (those who commit suicide).
− It is not made clear how the social disorganisation of an area is related to individual decisions to commit suicide.
− The ecological approach takes the suicide statistics at face value, when they are problematic.

Synoptic links

To other areas of the course
This approach relates in part to the sociology of work, where sociologists are interested in the effects of unemployment on the unemployed.

To methodological issues
This approach employs the classical sociological method of comparison, in this case between rural and urban areas and the suicide rates within them. Cavan, for example, compared the official statistics, including suicide, for 72 areas of Chicago to arrive at her conclusions.

To theoretical issues
This is a classical positivistic approach to an issue, relying on the official statistics to represent a real social phenomenon accurately. Anti-positivists would be critical of such an approach for ignoring individual motivations in committing a suicidal act.

Key concepts

Urban trend, community, social disorganisation, personal disorganisation, ecological fallacy.

Key thinkers

Cavan, Sainsbury, Weschler.

Interactionist approaches

Key ideas

- The official statistics on suicide are the product of social construction, through the actions of a large number of people.
- Deaths are not always easy to characterise as accidental, suicidal, natural or murder, and there is thus space for interpretation of an individual death by social agencies.

- Even to characterise a death as 'suspicious' is open to interpretation, with different social actors likely to view the same events in a different way.
- The crucial actor in the decision to define a death as suicide is the coroner, and coroners employ different 'rules of thumb' in coming to their decisions. Some sociologists therefore argue that we should reject suicide statistics as unreliable, others suggest that we should be sceptical about them, and still others argue for a limited acceptance as rough indicators of suicide rates.
- Moral factors intrude on the decision of key actors to define a death as a suicide or not: for example, Catholics are more reluctant to 'stigmatise' a death as suicide because of its sinful implications.
- Suicide does not therefore exist beyond the meaning that we, as social actors, give to it.

Evaluation

+ Interactionist approaches draw attention to the important social processes that underlie the creation of the suicide statistics.
+ They emphasise the ambiguity of all social actions, even seemingly obvious ones like dying.
+ They introduce the moral dimension into the sociological consideration of suicidal actions.
- The suicide statistics of a country do show remarkable stability across time despite the large number of individual decisions that have to be made to compile them.
- Any errors in the suicide statistics are random rather than systematic and therefore the statistics can be relied on to an extent.
- By rejecting statistics, interactionist approaches are removing the opportunity to discuss trends over time and comparisons between countries.

Synoptic links

To other areas of the course

The role of the doctor in defining particular acts as suicide, natural or suspicious focuses our attention on the power of the medical profession and the medical gaze in postmodern societies.

To methodological issues

The critique of the official suicide statistics is an exemplary case for dealing with all official statistics, no matter how hard or soft.

To theoretical issues

The interactionist emphasis on the meanings that individuals attach to a particular social action is central to action theory, delineating it from more structural theories such as functionalism and Marxism.

Key concepts

Social construction, coroners' definitions, soft statistics, suicidal acts.

Key thinkers

Cicourel, Taylor, Douglas, Atkinson.

Contemporary approaches

Key ideas

- Attempted suicides are not just failed suicides, but represent a different level of meaning from actions aimed at suicide.
- The meanings that can be attached to suicidal acts are much more varied than someone attempting to kill himself or herself.
- Attempted or failed suicidal acts have social consequences, involving support agencies, family, peers, work etc.
- It is often difficult to distinguish between those actions that are genuine attempts to end one's life, and those that are a cry for help.
- Many suicidal actions are 'gambles with death', in which the outcome of the action is uncertain and determined by factors out of the control of the 'suicide', such as chance discovery. They are therefore aimed at life and death at the same time.
- However, the actor can bias the outcome, through the method of suicide chosen, the location and the events leading up to and including the process of dying itself.
- Intentions can be inferred, but not completely known, through an examination of all the contingent circumstances surrounding the suicidal act.

Evaluation

+ Contemporary approaches have a more complex understanding of the nature and potential outcomes of suicidal acts.
+ They place the act of suicide into the social as well as personal circumstances surrounding it.
+ They refer to the consequences of the suicidal action and not just the causes.
− It is difficult to discuss trends in rates of suicide, given the uncertainty of outcome at the heart of these approaches.
− They compel the sociologist of suicide to examine each situation individually, with a resultant difficulty in drawing generalisations.
− Even a consideration of all circumstances leaves an element of the unknown in terms of intention.

Synoptic links

To other areas of the course

The issue of suicide can be linked both to the sociology of law, in that it has been subject to different legal constraints over the years, and to the issues of health and welfare, as the agencies that have to deal with the aftermath of a suicide attempt will include medical, psychological and social services.

To methodological issues

The problem of finding a method of accessing another's intentions is highlighted in these approaches. While the motivation for the suicide act may be expressed by the suicide themselves (in notes to friends etc.), whether the real intention was to die or to be discovered has to be gleaned from an examination of the circumstances in which the act took place.

To theoretical issues

The focus on inferring intentions provides a link to Weberian approaches to social life. Being 'adequate at the level of meaning' is a central tenet of Weber's approach.

Key concepts

Attempted suicide, gambles with death, contingent factors, intentions.

Key thinkers

Stengel, Taylor, Weiss.

Questions
&
Answers

This section provides you with three questions on the topic of **Crime and Deviance** in the style of the AQA unit test. The first two questions are followed by both a grade-A and a grade-C candidate response. You should note, however, that the grade-A responses are not 'model' answers and represent only one way in which the questions might be answered. You can use other material, adopt a different approach, make different synoptic links and come to a very different conclusion and still obtain very good marks. However, the answers do show you how to approach these sorts of synoptic questions generally. Like all responses at AS and A2, the candidate answers the question set, and not one that they would like to appear. The response demonstrates the skills that are required in the specification, including good written communication skills of spelling, punctuation and grammar. Thus, the best answers are critical and evaluative, use concepts appropriately and have a sound structure. They also make synoptic connections in line with the type of link identified in the italicised part of the question. The grade-C answers show a candidate who is on the right track, but who has made some errors or omissions that mean the response cannot obtain the highest marks.

The third question provided is for you to have a go at. Each part is accompanied by some advice to help you, and you can try to answer the question with or without reference to this advice.

Examiner's comments

The candidates' answers are interspersed with examiner's comments, preceded by the icon **e**. These comments will identify for you why high marks have been given and where improvements might be made, especially in the grade-C responses. You may wish to rewrite the grade-C answers to see if you can improve on the performance using the advice given.

Official statistics, the Chicago School and deviance amplification

Item A

The concept of the moral panic was first developed in Stanley Cohen's study of the 'mods and rockers' of the 1960s. These were rival youth groups which engaged in some minor violence in Clacton during the Easter weekend of 1964. The newspapers reported widespread violence and large numbers of arrests with such headlines as 'Day of Terror by Scooter Groups' (*Daily Telegraph*) and 'Youngsters Beat Up Town — 97 Leather Jacket Arrests' (*Daily Express*). These exaggerated reports generated public fear and a hostile reaction to the youth groups, which were seen as a major threat to public order. Mod and rocker subcultures received publicity, which led more teenagers to adopt these styles, further increasing public fear. Mods and rockers became what Cohen called the 'folk devils' of their time.

Source: Fulcher, J. and Scott, J. (1999) *Sociology*, Oxford University Press.

(a) **Discuss two ways in which it might be argued that official statistics of crime misrepresent the real rate of crime.** (8 marks)
This part of the question includes assessment of your understanding of the connections between Crime and Deviance and sociological methods.

(b) **Examine some of the strengths and weaknesses of the approach of the Chicago School to the study of urban crime.** (12 marks)
This part of the question includes assessment of your understanding of the connections between Crime and Deviance and sociological theory.

(c) **Using information from Item A and from other areas that you have studied, evaluate the importance of the mass media in the amplification of deviance.** (40 marks)
This part of the question includes assessment of your understanding of the connections between Crime and Deviance and other substantive topic(s) you have studied.

Total: 60 marks

■ ■ ■

Answer to question 1: grade-C candidate

(a) Many victims of crime do not report the events to the police because they are so minor, or they do not think that the police will be able to do much about them. Also, the way that the police patrol the streets affects the validity of the statistics, as they are much more likely to patrol in working-class areas and catch more criminals there. This produces bias in the criminal statistics.

While the candidate here has offered two acceptable reasons for misrepresentation in the criminal statistics (under-reporting and the effects of police patrols), the discussion of them is not well developed enough for an 8-mark question. This is a pity because the candidate does hint at being able to expand the points made into a good discussion, such as when he or she writes about bias in the statistics.

4/8 marks

(b) The Chicago School came out of Chicago where sociologists studied the distribution of crime according to the official statistics. The theory took the statistics as correct and showed that it was the slum areas of the city that were more likely to have high rates of crime. They found that cities were made up of concentric circles of housing from the central business district to the suburbs. There was a zone of transition in which crime was concentrated. The reason for this was that there was a culture of criminality passed on regardless of whether inhabitants moved on or stayed put, which meant that individuals were more likely to commit crime.

 Though not always clearly expressed, the broad outlines of the approach of the Chicago School are contained within the paragraph. The response is, as yet, only at the level of description rather than evaluation. It does, however, recognise that the Chicago School is a *theory* of crime and deviance.

The reason why crime is so high in these areas is that young people are not so supervised by older people and have greater opportunity to commit crime. It is particularly true of young men who are more likely to get in trouble with the law. They are often unemployed and hang around the street. They do not have the same attitude towards the law as mainstream society, because they do not come into contact with as many favourable attitudes towards the police as middle-class people do. As a result, they turn to criminal activity to get money or to gain status in their group.

 There are actually quite a number of valid points contained within this paragraph, but they are not always well developed. Description predominates and the candidate misses several opportunities to apply sociological concepts to what he or she is arguing, such as social disorganisation, subculture and differential association. Try to identify where these particular concepts might have been used.

A good thing about the theory is that it tries to show how cities grow 'naturally' and are organic. This means that there are different types of areas that occur in all cities. The criticism of this is that not all cities grow in this way and so it cannot be said to be a general theory of urban crime. It takes the official statistics as real, when they are not. It does not explain why some young men in the inner city become criminals and others in the same position do not. It does not explain all crime, such as murder. It just assumes that there is a criminal group in the inner city that passes on bad attitudes towards the police without showing that it did.

 This is a strange paragraph because it has many valid criticisms within it, but they are not always clear and they appear a little like a list of weaknesses. Each point should have been explained in greater detail to gain more AO2 marks. There is also an imbalance between the strengths and weaknesses, with only one real 'good thing'. As a result, the candidate has shown some AO2 skills, but would need to redress the balance and elaborate the points a little to gain a higher mark.

6/12 marks

(c) The role of the mass media in the amplification of deviance has been a concern of sociologists for some time. From the 1960s, when Cohen studied the mods and rockers, till today, with dole scroungers. The term amplification means something getting worse and here it refers to the ways in which newspaper reports can make an undesirable event worse. The work of Cohen on amplification suggested that the media's exaggeration of violence resulted in more violence actually being committed.

> Note that the second 'sentence' is actually not a full sentence. Remember that the quality of written work is also taken into account and you should be careful to write in full sentences at all times when writing essays. There is a fairly good, if basic, account of Cohen's views in this paragraph, although the last point made is open to different interpretations. Do you agree that 'amplification' means 'getting worse'?

There are various stages in the amplification of deviance. The first is where a group or an individual commits an antisocial action, such as a football hooligan. This is picked up by the media who report it to the public. Because of sensationalism, the public become concerned about the group and ask for more laws to deal with the problem. Politicians respond because they want to be popular. As a result of this process, a moral panic has been created about a folk devil.

> The description of the process could be much more firmly focused on the role of the media. For example, the candidate refers to sensationalism, but not in the context of the media. For example, how do the media sensationalise and why do they do it? To score synoptic marks, the connections to other areas of study should be explicitly made. This could also be done when the candidate writes about politicians. Similarly, the candidate applies appropriate concepts (moral panic and folk devil), but does not make connections to the media: for example, to the selection and presentation of media content, media representations, etc.

The media create folk devils through misrepresenting them in their reports. They produce accounts of people that make them appear a lot worse than they actually are. This is called stereotyping and journalists are responsible for doing this to certain social groups. Sometimes this involves the media in victim blaming, in that some vulnerable groups like asylum seekers are shown as frauds, when they may really be oppressed in their home country.

> This paragraph has some potential because it is seeking to apply some concepts to the issue of amplification and is focused on the role of the media. For example, stereotyping is deployed effectively here. Victim blaming is also used and is

supported by an example. However, this victim blaming could have been better explained than it is.

The media are not all bad. They do give us our knowledge of the world and without them we would not have such a great understanding of social events. The media are in competition with each other and there is a tendency to over-emphasise things which will sell newspapers. Nevertheless they do report real events, even if not always fully or with slight exaggerations.

e This paragraph is attempting to show that the media are not just about creating folk devils but also have some positive aspects. As such there is an evaluative edge to the paragraph, but it should be more clearly focused on the question set. Synoptic links are made in the first sentence with the topic of the Mass Media.

The process of deviancy amplification has been criticised by some sociologists. It is argued that the process is presented as a sort of automatic way in which the public respond to media reports, when sociologists such as McRobbie suggest that there are more complicated forces at work. For example, folk devil styles are often taken up by the fashion or culture industry and promoted as an alternative lifestyle rather than a deviant subculture. This idea is linked to the sociology of culture.

e There is an explicit synoptic link in this last sentence. Not only does this paragraph gain AO2 marks, but it also fulfils the requirement that connections are made to other areas of the course, through the reference to the core theme of culture.

The media are clearly involved in the process of deviancy amplification, amongst other things. By showing social groups in a particular light, it provokes a reaction from others, and this is demonstrated by many studies in this area such as Fishman's. This leads to more control over the folk devil group and also changes to the way in which the folk devils perceive themselves and behave. The end result is an increase in the originally reported deviance.

e As a conclusion, this contains some new information that would have been better contained in the main body of the answer. Nevertheless, it does score marks for knowledge and understanding. The candidate has taken a particular position on the evaluation of the process and supported it with reference to empirical material. A more sophisticated view of the processes involved would have been rewarded even more highly. In all, the answer would score 12 marks for AO1 and 10 marks for AO2.   **22/40 marks**

Overall: 32/60 marks

■ ■ ■

Answer to question 1: grade-A candidate

(a) The 'real' rate of crime is much larger than the recorded rate of crime for a number of reasons. The first is that many crimes remain 'invisible' to the recording authorities, although why this might be so will vary. A number of crimes are committed where the victims do not know that they are the victim of a criminal action, or where there are 'victimless' crimes. An example of the former is price-fixing by large cartels. It is not only difficult to prove that price-fixing goes on, but the buyers of the products are mainly ignorant of it and therefore do not make a complaint. Price-fixing is illegal because of competition laws designed to ensure that the consumer gets a fair deal. An example of 'victimless' crimes might be something like soliciting, where the prostitute and his or her client are consenting adults, who are unlikely to complain that the law is being broken.

🖉 This is a very good paragraph because it clearly lays out the first of two reasons and provides supporting discussion, including excellent examples to back up what is being argued.

The second reason why crime may go unreported is in how the police go about their business of catching and processing criminals. Again, this has many aspects that might result in a crime not being recorded as such. Williams showed that the police could not realistically process and record every minor crime that they come across during the course of their duties. For a start, the police officer does not know every law, so may see something that they are unsure about, in terms of its legality. Many minor offences are dealt with unofficially by the police officer as she or he tries to keep social order without criminalising every individual guilty of a minor crime. They may therefore choose to issue an unofficial warning rather than record the offence.

🖉 Following on the good start made in the first paragraph, the candidate here adds to the skills shown by applying a study to support the point being made. Notice also the use of the concept of 'criminalising' in an appropriate sociological way. The important thing about this answer is that it shows the candidate has a sophisticated understanding of the processes involved in the collection of criminal statistics.

8/8 marks

(b) The Chicago School approach to the reasons for the distribution of deviant and criminal behaviour in cities has been extremely influential on criminology over the years. It is based on the idea that the environment in which social groups live will influence their tendency to commit crime. The explanations given by the Chicago School arose from the observation that the official statistics of crime showed that it was concentrated in certain areas of the city (notably the zone of transition) and not others.

🖉 This is a very good opening paragraph, which begins with an evaluative point and then lays out the basic approach very succinctly. This is crucial because the marks for this part are weighted towards AO2 skills. While you have to show some knowledge of the approach in order to demonstrate its strengths and weaknesses, as the question asks, you should be concentrating on the AO2 skills of identification, analysis, interpretation and evaluation.

The Chicago School therefore tries to compare different areas of the city scientifically to establish the causes of crime, and Shaw and McKay come to the conclusion that it is the social organisation of the areas of high crime that is responsible. In particular, the nature of the community and networks in an area are important. Where there are strong communities and stable networks, social control is strongest and there is less incidence of crime. Where an area has a high level of social disorganisation, then crime is likely to be highest.

🖉 Again, the candidate describes the basic ideas of the Chicago School in a precise manner, getting to the very heart of their theory quickly. The candidate also introduces appropriately the central concepts of the Chicago School (community, network, social disorganisation) and a major piece of work (Shaw and McKay).

A strength of this approach is that it seems to follow the patterns of crime in city areas generally, in that most crime is recorded in inner-city areas. However, interactionists would argue that this seeming concentration in the zone of transition is a product of the way that the police patrol more heavily in these districts and systematically ignore or downplay middle-class crime. Moreover, other empirical work (Bottoms) did not confirm the conclusions of the Chicago School because it found that areas of cities with similar levels of social disorganisation had very different crime rates.

🖉 This is a good pattern to follow in answering this type of question. The candidate has identified a strength of the approach, but then shows some evaluative skills by discussing how this strength has been criticised by other perspectives and challenged by other empirical material.

The concept of social disorganisation is an important one in the study of deviance and crime and it has been influential on generations of sociologists interested in this area. It offers a social as opposed to an individual explanation of crime and is therefore linked to policies that seek to 'solve' the problem of crime through social change. For example, measures to improve the housing stock in inner-city areas are often done in a way that attempts to increase community spirit or that supports the idea of neighbourliness or reintegrative shaming. According to the Chicago School, an increase in these would bring down levels of crime.

🖉 This is a strong paragraph on the main strength of the approach. It establishes the Chicago School as a sociological approach and links this strength to policy attempts to affect the rate of crime. The candidate introduces the concept of reintegrative shaming, without really explaining it. There might have been another good point made here.

However, the concept of social disorganisation has come under some criticism for being, on the one hand, vague and on the other, moral. In the first case, while there are some indicators of social disorganisation suggested (levels of lone parents, divorce, rented flats, etc.), it is not clear how much of these indicators are needed to create social disorganisation. So, at what rate does divorce mean that an area is socially disorganised? It could also be argued that there is a middle-class moral disapproval in these indicators, which looks down on any arrangements that are different from the middle-class norm. Just because family arrangements in the inner city are different, it does not make them disorganised.

✍ The use of 'However' at the beginning of this paragraph indicates that there is going to be a contrast made to the previous paragraph and that we are now considering a weakness. Because the candidate is dealing with some complex issues here, they are not always expressed clearly, but they are sufficiently clear to score AO2 marks.

Therefore, the Chicago School has made a valuable contribution to the study of crime in establishing a proper role for its sociological study. But we must be careful not to accept all its ideas without being critical of them. It is quite an old explanation now and we should be looking for explanations that build on its ideas, while taking into account its weaknesses.

✍ The question only asks for 'some' of the strengths and weaknesses of the approach, so for 12 marks you are not expected to write a fully comprehensive account. This answer scores well because it addresses a couple of strengths and weaknesses in some detail and balances the answer between them. It also comes to an evaluative conclusion. **12/12 marks**

(c) To answer this question fully, we must draw upon sociological understandings of the mass media as well as deviance. The idea of deviancy amplification is firmly within the interactionist tradition and comes out of a consideration of the processes of labelling and self-fulfilling prophecy, which are important in the sociological study of deviance and education. Cohen developed the idea of the amplification of deviance spiral from his interest in the contradiction that the media often raged against deviant or criminal behaviour, but in so doing, often made the 'problem' worse. He was interested in the process whereby the media contributed to an increase in the very behaviour they were criticising.

✍ The opening sentence immediately recognises the synoptic demands of the question. It signals to the marker that the candidate has made the link to another substantive topic in sociology. The answer also makes a theoretical link which, though not a requirement of the question itself, does show that the candidate has a synoptic understanding. This is reinforced by the connection made through labelling to the area of education.

Cohen's work was concerned with the mods and rockers and some incidents on the sea-front one Bank Holiday. Although the original incidents were relatively minor — some scuffling and shoving and a lot of drunkenness — the papers chose to headline the violence as if it was much worse than it was. Cohen established this through content analysis of the newspapers. This kind of reporting created concern amongst the readers, the police and moral entrepreneurs in society and led to demands that something must be done about 'the young people of today'.

This concern is described by interactionists as a 'moral panic' about whoever is the 'folk devil' of the day. The media create folk devils all the time. The mods and rockers were in the 1960s, but today we might have asylum seekers. It does not even have to be an identifiable group. The European Union is presented as a folk devil by some papers.

> This paragraph is descriptive of Cohen's work and as half of the 40 marks available are for AO1 (knowledge and understanding), this is a good tactic by the candidate. There are also some AO2 marks to be awarded here, especially because he or she is making synoptic links as well. For example, look at the way that the candidate introduces the concept of headlining, which is normally associated with the study of the sociology of the media. There is a link to methodology made through content analysis. The paragraph also shows some good application skills in the use of examples — moving from the 1960s to contemporary society.

The effects of being labelled as a folk devil by the media are two-fold. It firstly changes the way that the police and the courts deal with the social group involved. For example, there was a greater police presence on the sea-front at the next Bank Holiday, with the result that more mods and rockers were caught doing violent things and so the problem seemed to be getting worse. It might mean, however, that no more violence was occurring, but the same level was noticed more. The second effect is that it changes the way the mods and rockers see themselves, so that they begin to take on the 'master status' of folk devil and act out their roles as the media have defined them. This is why it is often called a social reaction theory.

> Again, there is a good use of concepts here, such as master status. The focus of this paragraph is still description, but it draws upon deviance and media equally. Synoptic understanding is shown by the correct use of 'social reaction theory'.

There is some dispute about the implications of amplification amongst sociologists. Some argue that the media do actually create more deviance through their reporting, while others argue that the incidence of deviance does not increase, it is just the sensational reporting of the press that makes it look like there is an increase. It may be that there are different effects for different folk devils. For example, more young people might become mods and rockers when they read about it or see them on the television. Alexander argues that in the case of satanic abuse, there would not be a great rush to join such folk devil groups.

> There is quite a sophisticated debate going on here and the candidate demonstrates some good AO2 skills. The paragraph presents two sides of a sociological argument, but then shows that social life is much more complicated than a black-and-white debate would suggest. The candidate draws on the issue of 'media effects' from the Mass Media topic.

The idea of a deviancy amplification spiral has found much support from empirical studies of the media and deviant groups, for example smokers of marijuana. The process is one that strikes a chord amongst many people as an obvious way

in which the media construct concern amongst the public by choosing to emphasise and sensationalise particular events. However, it is also clear that the process
cannot be as automatic as sometimes presented. The media are actually made up
of a large number of gatekeepers, who control access to the making of the news
and who are unlikely to all follow the same stories. Indeed, many newspapers are
rivals and take different stands on issues to demonstrate their difference. So, they
do not always turn the same 'gaze' upon a group or event. Another problem with
the media side of the process is that it tends to assume that the audience for the
media reports all receive exactly the same message from the media. Yet, implicit
in the account is the idea that there are at least two different reactions to the
media accounts — the one from moral entrepreneurs and the public and the other
from the folk devils themselves. Why should there just be two ways in which the
media message can be interpreted?

🖉 We begin here to stock up some AO2 points and are moving on to evaluation.
There are some sophisticated points made in this paragraph and some inventive
use of concepts. Look at the way that the candidate uses 'gaze' to describe what
the media do. This idea is usually connected to the sociology of medicine or the
professions, so its use here is further evidence of synoptic links. The argument
presented about the audience is very well made and represents sophisticated
application and assessment skills. Material from the topic of the Mass Media is used
well and applied to the question.

So, to conclude, it may be that the media are an important avenue for the creation
of folk devils and moral panics, but it is not a straightforward road. The media are
not an undifferentiated agency and people do not respond to them in a deterministic way. People can use media reports for their own purposes — they can
even manipulate the media to create an image that they desire. It is also not clear
that our understanding of society can be separated from the media who are our
prime source of information. Yet certain social groups do come to be seen as
undesirable or a problem in society, and as we get our information about them
from the media rather than first hand, then it is likely that the media do play a
significant role in the process of deviancy amplification.

🖉 This comes to a good conclusion. Note that it does not really come down on one
side or the other. This is fine, especially as we are dealing with a very complex
process here. What the paragraph does do is lay out both sides of the debate and
alert the reader to the complex and unfinished nature of this debate. Clearly, we
have a very good answer here. It is both knowledgeable and skilful. There are some
issues that might have been included and some other pros and cons to be
discussed. In the time available, this does an excellent job of covering the issue and
scores 18 for AO1 and 17 for AO2. The synoptic element has been covered by a
comprehensive look at the media, with some mention of education.

35/40 marks

Overall: 55/60 marks

Interactionism, labelling, official statistics and ethnicity

Item A

A significant development in the sociology of deviance is labelling theory, a term often given to the symbolic interactionist perspective. Central to this is the wish to study the meanings and motives of the actor, and the meanings his or her actions have for society...There are some problems associated with the term labelling theory. In certain respects many different sociological theories are 'theories of labels' because they deal with negative or 'stigmatised' labels and how they affect the individual. The phrase 'labelling theory' will be used to refer to the particular branch of inter-actionist sociology concerned with how deviant labels are created, imposed and resisted through interaction.

Source: Kirby, M. et al. (1997) *Sociology in Perspective*, Heinemann.

(a) **Identify and briefly explain two strengths of the interactionist approach to crime and deviance.** (8 marks)

   This part of the question includes assessment of your understanding of the connections between Crime and Deviance and sociological theory.

(b) **With reference to Item A and any other area of social life you have studied during your course, discuss some of the disadvantages of labelling theory.** (12 marks)

   This part of the question includes assessment of your understanding of the connections between Crime and Deviance and other substantive topic(s) you have studied.

(c) **Assess the extent to which the official statistics on crime and ethnicity provide a valid picture of the criminal activities of ethnic minorities.** (40 marks)

   This part of the question includes assessment of your understanding of the connections between Crime and Deviance and sociological methods.

Total: 60 marks

■ ■ ■

Answer to question 2: grade-C candidate

(a) The two strengths of the interactionist approach to crime and deviance are labelling and relativism. The first shows that the way people have labels attached to them is an important part of the process of becoming a criminal. This is done usually by the police, the courts, the media and the public, or some combination of these. The second is that interactionists demonstrate that there is no such thing as deviance or crime. All there is are different ways of seeing the same events or people. What one group will see as terrorists, another will see as freedom fighters.

e This answer offers two acceptable strengths of the interactionist approach. The second one is an interesting answer because relativism is often used as a criticism of interactionism. However, the candidate has carefully explained why this is a strength and gives an example to back up the argument. Both points could have been expanded a little to score more highly. **4/8 marks**

(b) Labelling theory has been criticised in a number of different ways. Positivists argue that it is based on a wrong methodology. Structuralists argue that labelling theorists ignore important social factors which might cause crime and deviance, such as poverty, inequality and the like, and also ignore the original deviant act as if it was not real.

e There are some synoptic elements here in referring to the positivist and structuralist approaches. These theoretical criticisms are acceptable, but they could do with some exemplification to show the marker that the candidate really understands what is meant by these criticisms.

There is a difference between primary deviation and secondary deviation (Lemert). Primary deviation is the initial deviant action, such as breaking a window or truanting from school. This sort of thing everybody does at some time or another and it is not particularly remarkable. If you get caught when you do these things, you can then become a secondary deviant, because everybody knows you have done something wrong and they begin to act towards you as a vandal or a skiver from school. This might mean that your parents won't let you out at night because you might get into trouble again, or the teacher always assumes that you are 'wagging it' when you are really ill.

e The candidate is describing a basic idea behind labelling. While not always using sociological language, the candidate is demonstrating a good basic knowledge of the processes. There is also a synoptic dimension to this paragraph in the example of truanting from school, although this could be made more explicit.

Labelling theorists argue that your gender, class and ethnic origin are important in determining whether you are processed as a deviant or not by the police (secondary deviance). But it might just be that being known to the police or having a criminal record anyway might be more important. A more controversial view of labelling is that it treats those labelled as passive victims of the process with no say in it at all. This is odd for a theory that is supposed to be interactionist.

e There are a couple of criticisms in this paragraph, with the last one quite sophisticated. However, there is not enough criticism, given the question set, or sufficient reference to other areas of the course to score highly. **5/12 marks**

(c) The official statistics of crime and ethnicity do in the main provide a valid view of the criminal activity of ethnic minorities, although there are some problems with their collection and recording. The explanations that sociologists have put forward to account for the higher levels of crime amongst black young men vary according to perspective and willingness to accept the official statistics as real.

question

    The answer starts with a very strong statement about the relationship between the statistics and ethnicity, and in one sense tries to answer the question before any discussion. However, there is a qualification included at the end of the first sentence and at the end of the paragraph, which might allow some late focus on the methodological issue. We shall see!

Traditional explanations of ethnicity focused on the areas in which black people lived as an explanation for engaging more in crime. They looked at the social disorganisation of inner-city areas and concluded that it was the lack of community integration and the existence of weak social networks that led members of minority groups to commit more crime. The strain that ethnic minority groups felt in seeking to obtain the legitimate goals of society while being denied the legitimate means (Merton) meant that they turned to illegal activities. Ethnic subcultures grew up that were less favourable to the law and negative attitudes to law-abiding were passed down through generations.

    The paragraph offers an overview of sociocultural explanations of ethnicity and crime, including reference to Merton (interpretation skill). It would have been better if the candidate had explicitly described the traditional explanation's acceptance of the statistics as real, rather than just take it for granted.

Left realists argue that black people commit more crime because they are marginalised in society, through housing, lack of economic opportunity, and a loss of traditional masculine identity. They turn to illegal activities such as selling drugs, therefore, as a means of income support and also as a means of gaining status in their peer group. Because black youngsters experience prejudice and discrimination in society, they become frustrated and turn to violence to express this (Sellin).

    Again, there is a fair description of the realist approach, but there is little explicit reference to the methodological synoptic dimension of the question. The candidate is making synoptic links to theories, but the question requires a methodological discussion.

Social construction approaches argue that the official statistics are not real but are socially constructed through the activities of the police. Therefore by choosing to patrol certain areas of the city rather than others, the police ensure that there are more members of ethnic minorities caught. Once caught it is more likely that black as opposed to white men will proceed to trial, with white offenders gaining more cautions. In court, black people are more likely to be given a custodial sentence. This shows that it is not the case that black people commit more crime than white people, but that they are more likely to appear in the official statistics of crime because of the way that the criminal justice system operates.

    This is more focused because the candidate is using the social construction approach to explore the relationship between the official statistics of crime and ethnicity. There are some good evaluation points made as the processes of law enforcement are described.

Critical criminologists argue that it is part of the ideological and economic processes of capitalism to divide white from black workers and treat blacks as a reserve army of labour. This means that they are more likely to be made unemployed in times of difficulties and to turn to crime to make ends meet. Black people are defined as the 'Other' and seen as more likely to be criminal than the law-abiding host community. This is known as the new racism.

✒ Another theoretical approach is described here, making a synoptic link to theory but not directly addressing the issue of official statistics.

The way the relationship between official statistics and ethnic minorities is viewed therefore depends on the perspective adopted. Different sociologists explain the appearance of blacks in the crime statistics in different ways and one of those ways is the biased view of the official statistics.

✒ The conclusion seems a bit at odds with the opening sentence of the answer. The candidate has tried to tell a story about ethnicity and crime, but has chosen to list all the explanations she or he knows about this issue rather than really focus in on the methodological debate. Nevertheless, there is some discussion of the official statistics contained within the answer and the candidate demonstrates some good knowledge all the way through. The candidate therefore receives 13 marks for AO1 and 11 marks for AO2. **24/40 marks**

Overall: 33/60 marks

■ ■ ■

Answer to question 2: grade-A candidate

(a) The first strength of interactionist approaches to crime and deviance is that they draw our attention to the negotiated nature of both of them. Not only is what we see as deviant socially constructed, but so are the crime rates. For example, in different cultures, the same action will be seen in different ways. What might be a deviant form of family life in one society (plural marriages) might be seen as completely normal in another. In the case of crime, there are obviously different laws in different countries that will define certain acts such as murder in various ways. What might be legally murder in one country might be self-defence in another.

A second strength of the interactionist approach to crime and deviance is that it emphasises the roles of the social control agencies, such as the police and the courts, in the processes of creating deviance and criminality. This can take a number of varied strands, from the way that the law itself shapes social perceptions of right and wrong, to the way that the police operate in local communities. Similarly, the different ways that coroners deal with cases of suspicious death will affect the number of suicides, murders etc. that will appear in the official statistics of deviance.

question

> 🖉 Two distinct paragraphs cover a single strength each and they do it well. The focus of each paragraph is the first sentence, which lays out clearly what the strength is. The rest of each paragraph is geared towards expanding the initial point by giving examples or showing that there are multiple aspects to each point. However, the second paragraph is slightly weaker because the examples are not so well developed. For example, the point about the way the police operate would have been better made if an example of how they work in communities had been given. So, the addition of 'to target the activities of particular social groups, while ignoring others' would have been helpful. Nevertheless, this answer would still achieve a top-grade score. **7/8 marks**

(b) Labelling theory was developed initially by Becker to explore the ways that the social control agencies created deviants and criminals through their everyday activities. It was in opposition to the approach that saw the deviant population as somehow different to the mainstream population, and who could therefore be easily recognised and 'dealt with'. Becker argued that it was not any specific action that was inherently deviant, nor any particular group who were deviant. Rather, it was the activities of the police and courts (and the media some would argue) who attached the label of deviant to individuals and groups. Others, carrying out exactly the same activities, would not be labelled as deviant.

> 🖉 This is a good basic introduction to the work of Becker, which it is necessary to establish before the criticisms can be discussed.

The idea of labelling has also been applied in the sociology of education (Rosenthal and Jacobson), where the activities of teachers in labelling certain students as 'successes' or 'failures' have been argued to be one of the most important factors in the educational achievement of individuals. The idea is that, if teachers consistently apply a label to a student — for example 'clever' — then the student will come to believe that this is true and adopt the label as a 'master status'. The student will then begin to act in ways that conform to the master status, thus establishing a self-fulfilling prophecy.

> 🖉 This is a very clever paragraph because it does two things simultaneously. The most important thing is that it addresses the synoptic demands of the question — that links are made to other areas of the course. By using education as an example of the application of labelling, the candidate scores highly. But he or she also uses the opportunity of looking at education to introduce two other important concepts in labelling theory — master status and self-fulfilling prophecy. In passing, the paragraph also displays the sociological knowledge that the candidate has gained in his or her study of education, by the mention of Rosenthal and Jacobson.

However, critics of the labelling approach argue that the application of a label is assumed rather than empirically shown. For example, it is not clear how often a label has to be applied before it sticks. 'Does it have to be an official such as a police officer or a teacher who applies the label before the process kicks in?' critics ask. There is also the problem that the idea of a master status suggests that the label becomes the most dominant form of identity by the labelled. Those who oppose labelling suggest that there are many contradictory sources of identity available to individuals and it is unlikely that one of them becomes so dominant that it blocks out all others.

e There are two lines of critique here, both expressed at a level of sophistication that will attract reward. The candidate is applying some good concepts, such as identity, which is part of one of the themes of the A-level specification. This will also gain marks.

Lastly, the idea of a self-fulfilling prophecy has also come under attack. The argument is that acting in accordance with a label is just one of several outcomes that might come about. An equally likely reaction by an individual to being labelled 'thick' is to try and show the teacher who has done the labelling that he or she is wrong. This is known as the self-negating prophecy. Another reaction might be to ignore the label completely, because it is unimportant to the individual so labelled. This might be harder to do if it is the criminal justice system that is doing the labelling, as 'criminal' is a very public label to be landed with.

e This is signalled as the last criticism, remembering that there does not have to be a comprehensive critique for a 12-mark answer. But the candidate is careful to refer back to education in his or her example because that is the specific synoptic requirement of the question. Again, there is a level of sophisticated understanding shown here about the complexities of the labelling process and how it is not an automatic or deterministic process.

So, while labelling theory can be attractive to sociologists in looking at different areas of social life, it is not without its problems.

e Although this looks like a limited conclusion, it is fair enough because the question is asking not for an evaluation of labelling theory as a whole, but for a discussion of some of its criticisms. As a clearly synoptically driven answer, this would gain full marks. **12/12 marks**

(c) The picture presented by the official statistics on crime and ethnic minorities would consist of a concentration of criminality amongst certain sections of ethnic young males. This is known as disproportionate representation. It is particularly young black (Afro-Caribbean) males who are over-represented in the statistics of recorded crime and in the prison population, and South Asians (Indians, Pakistanis and Bangladeshis) who are under-represented. In approaching ethnicity and criminality, it is vital to categorise different ethnic groups separately rather than use a catch-all category such as 'Black' to include very different cultures and traditions.

e This first paragraph sets out very clearly the features of the official statistics to be discussed. Right from the start, the candidate has shown awareness of the danger of lumping all ethnic minorities together. There is a synoptic point about method-ology made at the end of the paragraph that sets the tone for the whole answer.

question

Allowing for differences in crime rates between ethnic groups, there does seem to be a statistical correlation between Afro-Caribbean young males and a higher rate of crime. But even this seeming straightforward connection is subject to criticism. For example, Morris (1976) points out that the official statistics that suggest this are based on the arrest rates of the police and not the actual amount of crime committed by different groups. When the evidence of self-report studies is taken into consideration, then the greater 'criminality' of young black men is less obvious, as roughly proportionate numbers of men from all backgrounds will report their crime. This suggests that the activities of the police in relation to young blacks need to be taken into consideration.

> There is good evaluation contained in this paragraph, made all the more powerful because it is supported with a reference to its source.

Another problem with taking the official statistics of crime and generalising to the population of ethnic minorities is the issue of multiple offending. If, for example, there was in the statistics a high concentration of offences in localities with a high concentration of ethnic minorities, it might be that there is only a small number of individuals engaged in lots of criminal activity. To say from this that ethnic minorities are more 'criminal' is to make a generalisation that is not supportable.

> Again, another telling criticism of taking the official statistics at face value is made in this paragraph. Marks are being gained for both the synoptic understanding shown and the complexity of the argument that is being built up.

There is thus a debate as to the real rate of criminal activity amongst the young ethnic population, especially Afro-Caribbeans. More sophisticated statistical analyses take into account many other factors when looking at ethnicity and crime. Stevens and Willis suggested that, even taking into account the activities of the police, there were higher levels of arrest for assault and robbery amongst Afro-Caribbeans. Other sociologists such as Cashmore argue that the reason young blacks appear more in the official statistics is because of hard policing of ethnic minority areas and institutional racism (Macpherson) amongst the police.

> This is a balanced paragraph showing the dispute between two points of view over the interpretation of the official statistics. This direct comparison of opposing points of view is a good technique for showing your evaluation skills. The paragraph would have benefited from an explanation of the reference to the Macpherson Report rather than just the mention of the name.

The routine activities theory can be applied to the way that the police try to police the population. It has been shown that there are stereotypes of black men held by the police that are likely to lead to more blacks than whites being stopped and searched, and more arrests of blacks made. The irony is that these stereotypes of greater criminality are likely to be developed in part as a reaction to the official statistics that show more blacks commit crime. By acting as if this was true, the police may arrest disproportionate numbers of black criminals rather than white criminals, thus creating a self-fulfilling prophecy. This can operate the other way as well, in that if South Asians are stereotyped as less criminal, they are less likely to be targeted by the police and thus less likely to appear in the statistics. Other sociologists, however, suggest that it is the greater community controls over young South Asians that make it more difficult for them to get in trouble.

There is a great deal in this paragraph and all of it is worthy, even if it does cover many points. The tone of the paragraph is evaluative and synoptic, applying the theory of routine activities to the over- and under-representation issue. The reappearance of South Asians in this paragraph shows that the candidate has followed through on her or his points in the initial paragraph.

To conclude, there is a problem with the statistics that show the relationship between ethnic minorities and crime. That problem is the issue of validity. Do the official statistics show the real rate of criminal activity amongst ethnic minorities and therefore show a greater criminality among Afro-Caribbeans and a lesser criminality amongst South Asians? If they do, then it will help society and the forces of law and order to use their resources to combat crime in a more efficient way. If they do not, then it could be that the statistics are reinforcing institutional racism and unfairness to certain ethnic groups. From a sociological point of view, the use of official statistics is also important because accepting them as valid or not will affect the types of explanations that the sociologist would look for. I do not think that the statistics tell the whole story of ethnicity and crime and they should therefore be treated with caution.

This is a concluding paragraph of merit. It applies the concept of validity well to attempt to come to a conclusion, and at the end the candidate lays out what she or he thinks about the issue (evaluation). This is fine because the opinion is based on the evidence laid out in the body of the answer. However, the sociological support (studies and sociologists) is less well developed. There is a sophisticated understanding being demonstrated here, but it is the AO2 skills that shine through. The answer is also due for a high mark because it keeps its focus on the issue of statistics and ethnicity as required by the question. It thus gains 16 marks for AO1, but 20 for AO2. **36/40 marks**

Overall: 55/60 marks

uestion 3

Social factors, participant observation and interactionism

Item A

Sociologists have long recognised the centrality of the idea of culture when approaching the issues of crime and deviance. The implicit contrast here is between sociological explanations, which rely on culture as their basis, and the biological emphasis that influenced the development of criminology as a discipline.

If culture is defined as all the ideas, values, emotions and attitudes that shape and constrain individual behaviour in society, then it can be seen that the culture of that society will be important in defining which behaviours are acceptable and which are not.

Source: adapted from Lawson, T. and Heaton, T. (1999) *Crime and Deviance,* Macmillan.

(a) **With reference to Item A and using examples from any other part of the course, discuss two social factors that sociologists suggest may lead to deviant behaviour.** (8 marks)
This part of the question includes assessment of your understanding of the connections between Crime and Deviance and the other substantive topic(s) you have studied.

(b) **Examine some of the problems that might be encountered in using participant observation in the study of girl gangs.** (12 marks)
This part of the question includes assessment of your understanding of the connections between Crime and Deviance and sociological methods.

(c) **Evaluate interactionist approaches to the study of crime and deviance.** (40 marks)
This part of the question includes assessment of your understanding of the connections between Crime and Deviance and sociological theory.

Total: 60 marks

■ ■ ■

Answer this synoptic question, making sure that you employ all the concepts, ideas and sociologists suggested in the following:
(a) material deprivation, social disorganisation, Gartner, Shaw and McKay, zone of transition, unemployment, family dissolution, community networks
(b) Hawthorne effect, halo effect, ethical dimension, entry, exit, criminal involvement, gender dimension, naturalism
(c) labelling, Becker, primary deviance, secondary deviance, master status, deinstitutionalisation, amplification of deviance, Braithwaite, shame and reintegration, Gove, postmodernism, self-control, opportunity, Henry and Milovanovic